ANALYSIS THROUGH COMP

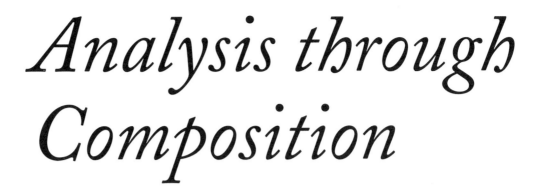

Analysis through Composition

Principles of the Classical Style

NICHOLAS COOK

OXFORD

UNIVERSITY PRESS

OXFORD
UNIVERSITY PRESS

Great Clarendon Street, Oxford OX2 6DP
Oxford University Press is a department of the University of Oxford.
It furthers the University's objective of excellence in research, scholarship,
and education by publishing worldwide in
Oxford New York
Auckland Cape Town Dar es Salaam Hong Kong Karachi
Kuala Lumpur Madrid Melbourne Mexico City Nairobi
New Delhi Shanghai Taipei Toronto
With offices in
Argentina Austria Brazil Chile Czech Republic France Greece
Guatemala Hungary Italy Japan South Korea Poland Portugal
Singapore Switzerland Thailand Turkey Ukraine Vietnam

Oxford is a registered trade mark of Oxford University Press
in the UK and in certain other countries
Published in the United States
by Oxford University Press Inc., New York

British Library Cataloguing in Publication Data

Data available

Library of Congress Cataloging in Publication Data

Cook Nicholas, 1950-
Analysis through composition : Principles of the Classical style/
Nicholas Cook.
1. Music–18th century–Theory   2. Style, Musical.
3. Musical analysis   I. Title.
MT6.C775A53   1996   781–dc20   94-44695

ISBN 0-19-879013-9

10 9 8 7

Set by Hope Services (Abingdon) Ltd.
Printed by Golden Crown Printing Co., Ltd.
on acid-free paper

Contents

About This Book

To the best of my knowledge there isn't another book quite like this. So it requires some explanation. I shall try to offer this by answering three questions. They are:

- What is it for?
- Who is it for?
- How can it be used?

What is it for?

The basic principle behind this book is that many practical musical activities involve analysis, otherwise known as musical intelligence. For example, when Beethoven arranged his Piano Sonata Op. 14 No. 1 for string quartet, he didn't transcribe the music mechanically, one note at a time: that would have shown a complete lack of musical intelligence. Instead, he stripped off the piano figuration, and recast the tunes and harmonies in a manner appropriate for strings. That is to say, he discarded what was decorative and kept what was essential. He was performing a kind of analysis, even though it was carried out in purely practical terms.

The purpose of this book is to create an environment of varied musical activity that will inculcate and nurture basic analytical concepts in a practical context. It is organized round a series of assignments that involve (among other things) writing arrangements, realizing accompaniments, composing variations, and expanding small pieces into larger ones. It also involves writing some analyses. But the idea is to keep the analysis linked as closely as possible to the music. It is to my mind a mistake to introduce abstract music-analytical concepts at too early a stage in the educational process: students whose musical experience may be quite limited all too easily adopt an over-cerebral approach to analysis, seeing it as a kind of mathematical activity with no direct link to the experience of making or listening to music. (This is further reinforced by traditional rule-based approaches to harmony and counterpoint.) It is much better, I think, to encourage the development of a basic analytical approach in the context of practical musical activity, and then at a subsequent stage to refine and generalize this approach through the teaching of more formalized theory.

Much of the musical activity to which I have referred involves composition. But this book is not intended to teach composition; as the title indicates, it is intended to teach analysis *through* composition. In other words, composition is the means rather than the end of the learning process. In Britain, much more than in North America, there is a tradition of teaching students to compose in historical styles (sometimes called 'pastiche composition'). This has its origins in nineteenth-century historicism, on the assumption that composers would learn their craft through imitation of the most approved masters of the past. Few people, if any, believe nowadays that this is how composers find their voice; I certainly don't subscribe to that belief. To be sure, postmodernist composers, and practically all composers working in the commercial sector, need a good grounding in common-practice styles, so maybe this book will have something to offer them. But that is tangential to its main aim.

The basic stance of this book might be called integrationist. It integrates disciplines, or sub-disciplines, that are often taught separately: harmony, counterpoint, composition, analysis, and theory. More broadly, it tries to integrate music with the context of its production: hence the inclusion of topics such as how late eighteenth-century composers learnt their craft, the sketching process, and revision. I aim to achieve two things by this. One is to make the assignments reasonably realistic in nature; most of them involve doing things that apprentice composers actually did in the late eighteenth century (so there are no assignments consisting of Haydn quartets with passages blanked out). The other, and more important, aim is to provide a foundation for the study of music history. The idea is to bring about what, in the Conclusion, I call a 'composer's-eye view' of the Classical repertory. Once you have some hands-on experience of how the music was made, you are in a much better position to understand its historical development or relate it to its social context. In short, you can appreciate it as a human product.

This ties in with the limitation of the repertory with which this book deals: European music of the early Classical period, from the 1760s to just before 1800. The reason for limiting the scope to *this* period is fairly self-evident: it offers music that is easy to play, manageable in length, clear in organization, and familiar in style. But why limit it at all, when the music of practically all times and places is no further away than the nearest library or record store? The reason is that only if you deal with a restricted repertory is it easy to develop fluency in dealing with it—to internalize its principles and conventions, in the way you know your native language. You can get *inside* the style in a way that is impossible when you jump about, however invigoratingly, from Bach to Boulez to the Beatles and Balinese gamelan (and back). And what is more, once you have developed a composer's-eye view of one style of music, you can readily transfer it to other styles; though the subtitle of the book is 'Principles of the Classical Style', I would like to think that it offers a foundation for understanding a far broader and perhaps unlimited range of musics. In this way, I do not see the narrow repertory focus of this book as antithetical to the broad vision, the valorization of diversity, that characterizes today's thinking about music. On the contrary, I see the two approaches—the broad and the narrow—as complementary elements in a well-designed curriculum.

Who is it for?

As may be obvious from its format, this book is primarily intended for teachers and students of music at undergraduate level. It does not teach music from scratch; it assumes some familiarity with the rudiments, including for instance the concepts of scale, key, and mode, as well as basic harmonic functions. The opening chapters include a rapid survey of such topics as diatonic harmony, Roman letters, and harmony versus non-harmony notes. But they are intended primarily for the purposes of reviewing previously-encountered concepts, rather than of introducing them for the first time.

This strategy is in part explained by the changing circumstances of music education in Britain during the 1990s—changes which have to a greater or lesser extent been matched elsewhere. Until the late 1980s, the public examinations in music taken between the ages of 15 and 18 were designed, so to speak, backwards from first-year university music courses; they supplied a solid foundation in harmony and counterpoint through the intensive study of Bach-style chorale harmonization, two-part inventions, and so forth. Over a period of years these traditional curricula were swept away and replaced by new ones which were far more student-centred in conception, aiming not only to develop students' capacities across a range of activities (composing, performing, appraising) but also to introduce them to the wide diversity of musics that characterizes modern society: pop, jazz, world, and of course classical, to name only a few.

Inevitably the inclusion of new elements has gone hand-in-hand with a decline in terms of traditional skills; it is not so much that these skills are no longer taught, but they are taught in less depth and there is a wide range of knowledge among students who have followed different syllabuses. Through providing a review of basic concepts of harmony and counterpoint, the initial chapters of this book are designed to enable students who have not covered these areas to be identified and offered appropriate training. But that is not their only purpose. They are also intended to lead students who *are* familiar with these areas towards a more reflective, analytical way of thinking about them. Through this process of reorientation, these chapters lay the foundations for the integrationist and historically-aware approach on which the book is predicated.

The basic expectation, then, is that before beginning on this book students will have had something like a year's experience of basic theory, incorporating diatonic and perhaps some chromatic harmony, Roman-letter analysis, and elementary counterpoint. (If they have had some exposure to figured bass as well, then so much the better.) But by including reviews of all these topics, together with a glossary and a schematic overview of Classical harmony, I hope to have made the entry point as flexible as possible. Indeed, it is possible to imagine the book being introduced at an earlier stage in the curriculum, providing an overall framework for the teaching of basic theory, but being supplemented by other texts as required. In this case, the most important supplement would probably be a keyboard harmony manual; I think that basic harmony is best taught at the keyboard whenever possible, and the initial chapters of this book can be used in tandem with a text like *A New Approach to Keyboard Harmony* (see the Introduction to Part I).

How can it be used?

This book takes the form of an integrated course lasting approximately one year, and includes a range of assignments for students to complete (for which worksheets are provided when appropriate). As you might guess, it has its origins in a course which worked in precisely that way. But I hope that the materials will also be found of value when used selectively, that is to say that teachers will pick and choose from them in the context of their own course structures. Other teachers may not wish to use the materials directly, but find the book of interest as an ideas bank. Finally, I hope that it will have some appeal outside the strictly pedagogical context, to students and other readers who may be stimulated by the approach to Classical music that it offers.

In the remainder of this section, I shall try to explain the sequencing of the materials in the book, and make some suggestions (based on my own experience) as to how it may be used within the context of an integrated course.

Sequencing of materials

The introductory chapter focuses on a single page of music (from a sonata by J. C. Bach), setting out an analytical approach to the movement, and at the same time offering a review of basic theoretical concepts; the idea of reduction makes its first appearance here, though readers are not at this stage expected to make their own reductions. Chapters 1 and 2 are designed to develop further the analytical approach through the practical activities of arrangement and accompaniment. Chapter 2 stresses the need to pick out the essential harmonic changes in accompaniment, and uses this to introduce the idea of using Roman letters selectively rather than mechanically; this is an example of what I mean by integrating theory and practice. Chapters 3 to 5 focus on phrase structure, two-part counterpoint, and chromatic harmony, and culminate in an examination of Mozart's composition teaching, as revealed by the Attwood notebook. The assignments in Chapter 5 are largely Mozart's own.

Up to this point the aim has been to introduce what might be called the basic vocabulary and syntax of Classical music. The following four chapters (6 to 9) introduce essential compositional techniques. Among these are variation (for both keyboard and orchestral instruments), and what I describe as the two complementary techniques of expansion. One of these is the modular principle, whereby a phrase of music is divided into fragments which are repeated and reconfigured in new ways; my account at this point follows Heinrich Koch's *Introductory Essay on Composition*. The other is the principle of prolongation, which I illustrate through analysing cadenzas; this leads naturally to a refinement of the reduction technique introduced in the earlier part of the book, and Chapter 9 includes what is in its essentials a Schenkerian analysis. I don't expect readers to be able to prepare their own Schenkerian analyses (though by the end of the book they should be in a good position to begin formal Schenkerian studies, if desired); but they should be able to *follow* one, at least as far as the middleground.

The final chapters (10 to 12) focus on sonata first-movement form, showing how the various compositional techniques are used together to create substantial pieces of music. They take the form of a series of analytical case studies, which have been selected with a view to the kind of integration between analysis and contextual study that I mentioned earlier. So Chapter 11 offers a comparison of two Mozart sonata movements, one of which (KV 284) exists in an abandoned draft version; it has also been the subject of a 'topical' analysis by Leonard Ratner. And Chapter 12 shows how analysis helps to make sense of Beethoven's sketches for his little Sonata Op. 49 No. 2; the selection of this piece is intended to allow a smooth transition, if desired, to the more extensive analysis of the same movement in my *Guide to Musical Analysis* (London and New York, 1987).

Each of the four parts into which the book falls has its own introduction, outlining the essential issues and offering suggestions for further study.

One way of using it

The purpose of what follows is not, of course, to specify how the book *should* be used, but simply to provide an example of how it *can* be used.

This book is based on a Music Foundation course for first-year music undergraduates at the University of Southampton, lasting two semesters (twenty-four teaching weeks). That allows two weeks per chapter, including the Introduction, but excluding the final chapter, an assignment which can be set as an end-of-year project. The course can be presented by means of formal lectures, but it works best when these are supplemented by small group tutorials; in many institutions the only affordable means of delivering small group teaching is through the use of postgraduate teaching assistants, and one of the advantages of a book like this is that it provides the coordination that is necessary under such circumstances. Small group teaching also makes it possible, where appropriate, to integrate keyboard harmony and aural training with the course—skills which, as I see it, are acquired most effectively when they form part of a coherent programme of music learning.

I have provided more assignments than are actually required, and this makes it possible to some extent to weight the selection towards either composition or analysis. (I try to keep a balance between the two.) There are just a few assignments which are really intended for self study rather than for formal submission and evaluation: an example is Assignment 30 where it would be relatively easy for students to track down the original music and copy it out. The vast majority of the assignments, however, pose no such problems; this is one of the advantages of asking students to reconstruct parts of compositions that really *are* lost, rather than blanking out sections of a score that can be found in the nearest library!

Wherever it seems most useful, and particularly in the earlier part of the book, worksheets are provided for student use; these will be found at the end of the book, and the symbol □ is used within the text to indicate the presence of one. Worksheets have a number of advantages: they clarify what is wanted, particularly in the early stages; they save students unnecessary copying; and they ensure that answers are provided in a clear and consistent format. This last point is an important one whenever the instructor's time is at a premium (and when isn't it?), because it maximizes throughput in evaluation.

PHOTOCOPYING OF WORKSHEETS

When this book is adopted for a class, the ideal arrangement is of course that each member of the class has his or her own copy of it. In this case the worksheets, when used, may be removed and submitted to the instructor for evaluation.

However it may not always be practical for each member of the class to purchase a copy. For this reason, unlimited copying of worksheets is permitted, and no fee is payable in respect of this. As the assignments generally require reference to the text and/or to music examples in the text, it will of course be necessary for copies of the book to be available for student reference.

Acknowledgements

Michael Rogers and Kofi Agawu both made extremely helpful comments on drafts of this book, for which I am grateful; Michael and an anonymous publisher's reader both made suggestions as to the title, and I simply took one of their suggestions for the title and the other for the subtitle. I would like to thank Ric Graebner and Hannah Vlcek, who co-taught the course for which this book was written at the University of Southampton, and picked up many mistakes and infelicities in the process. And of course I would like to thank the guinea-pigs, that is to say the students in Hong Kong and Southampton on whom these materials were tried out.

Thanks are due to the following copyright-holders for permission to reproduce musical materials: Bärenreiter-Verlag (*Neue Mozart-Ausgabe*); The British Library ('Attwood' Notebook; Beethoven, 'Kafka Miscellany', including transcription by Joseph Kerman); Verlag Doblinger (Haydn, *Divertimento a Sei* Hob. II:11); Unión Musical Ediciones, S.L. (Soler, Sonata Op. 8 No. 3); G. Henle Verlag (Haydn, *Divertimento in C*, Hob. XIV: 10); Bibloteka Jagiellonska (abandoned autograph of Mozart's Sonata KV 284, first movement); Stiftung Mozarteum Salzburg (autograph of Mozart's *Lobgesang auf die feierliche Johannisloge*); Orszagos Széchény Könyvtar (Mozart, *Modulierendes Präludium*).

Checking the proofs of this book has made me realize how many mistakes must remain. Corrections and other suggestions which might be incorporated in a future edition of this book will be gratefully received, and should be addressed to the author, c/o Oxford University Press.

This book is dedicated to Peter Evans, who introduced me to the integrated approach to music theory that I have tried to develop in it.

Music Sources

Examples

56   *NMA* X/30/1, p. 197.

58–9   *NMA* X/30/1, pp. 201, 216.

60   *NMA* VIII/20/1/1.

61   KV 168ᵃ; *NMA* VIII/20/1/1.

62   *NMA* X/30/1, pp. 175–6.

63   *Diletto Musicale*, 57.

65   *NMA* IX/26.

70   Op. 5 No. 3, II.

71   *Werke* XVIII/1/1. The *Divertimento in A* Hob. V:7 is in *Werke* XI/1/1.

72   *NMA* IX/26.

74   *NMA* III/8.

75   *NMA* IX/27/1.

77   *NMA* IX/27/1, p. 175.

78–80   Adapted from Koch, *Introductory Essay* (Part 2, Section 3).

81   Adapted from Koch, *Introductory Essay*, Exx. 278, 281, 284, 323.

84   *NMA* IX/27/2, pp. 4–5.

86–9   *NMA* IX/26.

92–3   As Exx. 86–9.

96   Sonatine Op. 6, reprinted in F. Giegling, *The Solo Sonata* (Arno Volk Verlag, Köln, 1960).

97   *NMA* IX/25/2, p. 173.

104   *NMA* IX/25/1.

105   P. S. Rubio (ed.), *P. Antonio Soler, O.S.H.: Sonatas para Instrumentos de Tecla* (Unión Musical Ediciones, S.L., Madrid, 1962), Vol. 6.

107   J. Kerman (ed.), *Ludwig van Beethoven: Autograph Miscellany from circa 1786 to 1789*.

112   As Ex. 107.

Worksheets

11   'Lied der Sophie' from *Der Bergknappen*; *DTÖ* XVIII/1 (=36).

12   KV 315ᵃ, Nos. 2, 3; *NMA* IV/13/1/1.

14   Koch, *Introductory Essay*, Exx. 191, 70a.

16   Koch, *Introductory Essay*, Exx. 248, 247, 249.

18   Koch, *Introductory Essay*, Ex. 286.

22   *NMA* X/30/2, p. 37.

24–5   *NMA* X/30/2, pp. 19, 23.

28   *NMA* X/30/2, p. 17.

35   *NMA* IX/27/1.

36   Koch, *Introductory Essay*, Exx. 287, 339; Haydn, *Werke* XVIII/1/1.

INTRODUCTION

A Page of Music

Example 1 shows a page of music, the Minuet from Johann Christian Bach's Sonata, Op. 5 No. 2. Like all music, it is not just something to play; it is a historical document as well.

The very fact that it appeared in this published form reflects the circumstances of Bach's life. Son of Johann Sebastian, and younger half-brother of Carl Philipp Emanuel, Johann Christian took up residence in London in 1762. There he established himself as a keyboard player and teacher as well as composer, and was soon the most fashionable musician in the capital. Within months of his arrival he began publishing keyboard music, which found a ready market. During this period, music was undergoing a tremendous expansion among the middle classes. The piano, a new invention, was considerably cheaper to buy than the harpsichord. It became an essential part of the middle-class household, a kind of home entertainment centre. It also became a vehicle

Ex. 1 J. C. Bach, Sonata Op. 5 No. 2, Minuet (London, 1766)

for social aspiration: playing the piano was a social accomplishment, particularly for young women. And this is where J. C. Bach came in. As Charles Burney put it a few years later in the second volume of his *General History of Music* (London, 1782), Bach's 'compositions for the piano forte are such as ladies can execute with little trouble'. Bach's Op. 5 played a key role in opening up this domestic market.

Music like J. C. Bach's Op. 5 was a luxury commodity; it was handsomely engraved and bound, and compared with other items it was a great deal more expensive than music is today. But why the horizontal format? In 1766, when Op. 5 was published, there was nothing unusual about this. Although the upright format of present-day editions was sometimes used for keyboard music in Bach's time, the horizontal format (today standard only in piano duet and organ music) was more common—both for published music and for composers' manuscripts. It is easy to see why; its long lines helped to make the musical process readily visible in a way that today's upright-format editions do not. Even after the upright format became standard for published music, around 1800, many composers continued to prefer the horizontal one for their manuscript paper; most of Beethoven's and Schubert's sketches and autographs are laid out this way.

With its elaborately calligraphic lettering, the title page of Op. 5 lends prestige to the music (**Example 2**; according to the inscription, this was a presentation copy). More practically, it says that the music is 'for the Piano Forte or Harpsichord'. There were sound commercial reasons for saying this: although the piano was gaining ground all the

Ex. 2 Title page of 1766 edition of Bach's Op. 5

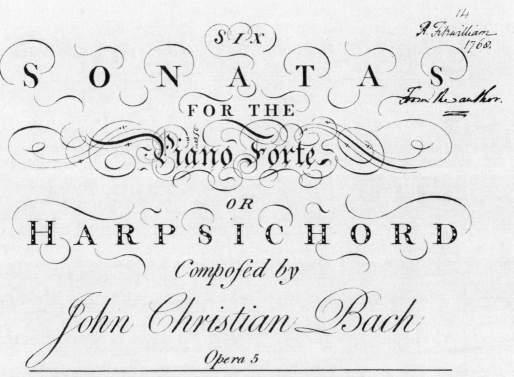

time, there were still a considerable number of harpsichords in use in 1766. And certainly the Minuet from Op. 5 No. 2 works well enough on the harpsichord. As you can see from the reset version in **Example 3** (which includes bar numbers for ease of reference), it contains just one dynamic marking, the 'P°—for 'piano'—in bar 29. This comes at the beginning of the *Minore* (minor-mode) section, and if you were playing the piece on a two-manual harpsichord, you could play the whole of this section on the other manual with a quieter stop, going back to the original manual for the repeat of the first section ('*Da Capo il Maggiore*', 'from the beginning of the major section'; throughout the Classical period, Italian was the common language of professional musicians). But there are other pieces in Op. 5 that would not work on the harpsichord. The third sonata, for instance, demands rapid alternations between piano and forte, while the first includes a crescendo marking. Despite the title page's claim, then, these pieces are really for piano.

The music in Examples 1 and 3 is the second movement of a two-movement *sonata* and it carries a title: *Minuetto*. That's not simply a name; it says something about the music, setting up a particular set of expectations. The minuet was a rather graceful dance in ternary metre, something like the nineteenth-century waltz but without its characteristic swing. That doesn't mean that Bach expected people to dance to this minuet. Eighteenth-century composers often liked to evoke the characteristics of a particular dance, even when they were writing music that was simply for playing or listening to. So the title tells us to expect a piece that creates an impression of graceful, unhurried, measured movement; equally, it tells the performer to play the music that way.

Can we be more precise about how the music creates this impression? Like most dance music, Bach's minuet falls into fairly regular sections, with the overall effect deriving largely from the balance or symmetry between the various sections. Imagine that you were playing the melody line of Example 3 on a wind instrument: where would you breathe? The answer is surely every four bars—that is, at the end of bars 4, 8, 12, and so on. (Breathing anywhere else would create a chopped-up, incoherent effect.) What is it about the music that makes this the natural thing to do? There are rests at the end of bars

A NOTE ON TERMINOLOGY

Bernard Shaw, the playwright, once said that Britain and North America are divided by a common language. That certainly applies to music, where there are a number of basic terms that are different. The most important are:

- Bars (British) or measures (American). In this book I call them bars.

- Rhythmic values. Americans refer to these mathematically, while the British give them traditional names. In this book I use the American terminology. The equivalances are as follows:

American	British
Whole note	Breve
Half note	Minim
Quarter note	Crotchet
Eighth note	Quaver
Sixteenth note	Semiquaver
Thirty-second note	Semidemiquaver

8, 12, and 16, so that's one indication. And it's obvious that there is a break at the end of bar 8, and again at the end of bar 28, because at each point you go back and repeat the section (hence the double bar lines, which help to make the music's organization visible at a glance). But there are other places (bars 4 and 24) where nothing at all is marked, and yet it's just as *musically* obvious that these are good places to breathe. Why is this?

The answer has to do with harmonic structure. Now harmonic structure is a technical matter, and we need a technical terminology to deal with it. Although they weren't used in Bach's time, *Roman letters* (otherwise known as Roman numerals) are commonly used today as a means of analysing harmonic structure—that is, of saying what the chords are and how they relate to one another. The last point is crucial: Roman letters are all about relationships. They relate (or rather, they allow *you* to relate) any given chord to its *root*, and in turn they relate this root to the *tonic*; as you can see from

Ex. 3 J. C. Bach, Sonata Op. 5 No. 2, Minuet

Minuetto

Da Capo il Maggiore

Example 4, the Roman letter is actually a measure of the distance between the root and the tonic, counting upwards from the tonic. So if you have a chord progression such as II–V–I, the Roman letters don't relate each chord directly to the next. In effect, they are saying that how two chords sound in relation to one another depends on how each of them sounds in relation to the tonic.

In order to apply Roman letters to a given passage of music, then, you have to make three decisions:

- What is the root?
- What is the tonic?
- What is the distance between the root and the tonic?

Ex. 4

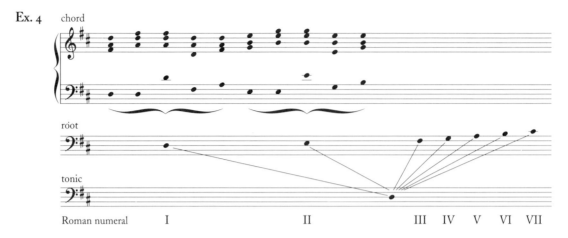

The last of these doesn't require further commentary: it's just a matter of arithmetic. But the other questions are not always as straightforward as they might seem. The opening of Example 3 illustrates this. First of all, what is the tonic? The key signature indicates either D major or B minor, and the fact that the movement ends in D major makes it quite clear that D is the tonic. That's straightfoward enough. But what about the root of the first chord?

Here we encounter the first problem in applying Roman letters to real music. In the harmony textbooks, as in my Example 4, you find complete *triads*. And there are clear rules for deciding what the root of any triad is. (In short, you stack up the notes of the triad in thirds, ignoring the *register* in which they appear; the bottom note of the stack is the root. If you can't stack the notes this way, you're not dealing with a triad.) But in real life composers don't always use each note of the triad: sometimes they use just two notes, and sometimes only one. This is what happens on the very first beat of Example 3, which simply consists of two Ds an octave apart. Similarly, on the second beat, we have just two notes—an E in the right hand, and a C♯ (which moves down to A on the next beat) in the left. In cases like this, there isn't an automatic rule for deciding what the root is; you have to use your own musical judgement.

On the first beat it's perfectly clear that the root is D, giving a tonic chord (I); this is partly because the root is the least likely note to be omitted, and partly because it is usual for music like this to begin with a tonic chord. But things aren't so straightforward on the second beat. Since the C♯ in the bass coincides with an E in the melody, it would seem logical enough to assume that the C♯ is the root, so that the chord is a VII with its fifth omitted. Similarly, on the third beat, the A in the bass coincides mainly with Es in the melody (I'll talk about the D later), so this time the obvious interpretation is V. That gives us a progression I–VII–V for the whole bar. That's not a very familiar progression. But there's a more serious problem than that. If we read the bar as I–VII–V, then we are saying there is a regular pattern of harmonic change throughout it. And that's not really true. There is a definite feeling of chord change, of one chord replacing another, between beats 1 and 2. But there isn't any such feeling between beats 2 and 3; it's as if the VII and V were continuous with one another. In fact they sound like the same chord. And we can reflect this in the Roman-letter analysis, by interpreting the C♯ not as the root of a VII chord, but as the third of a V. In other words, we can understand the harmony of the bar as I–V, with a single chord change on beat 2, and with the V chord appearing in first *inversion* on beat 2 and in *root position* on beat 3. Mathematically speaking, this analysis isn't any more correct than the I–VII–V one; musically speaking, however, it certainly is.

Ex. 5

Example 5 continues this analysis for the whole of the first four bars. (It contains an additional and very common harmonic symbol: V⁷ or the dominant *seventh*, a V chord with an added seventh above the bass.) You can see that I have put rings round a lot of the notes in the right-hand part. This is to show that they are not *harmony notes*. There is very little Classical music that consists simply of one chord after another. Almost always, and particularly in melodic writing, there are notes that do not belong to the harmony but weave in and out of it. There are various ways in which this can happen, and the letters above the ringed notes in Example 5 illustrate the most important ones. They are:

- *Passing notes* (P). These connect two harmony notes. In the top line of bar 2, for instance, the F♯ and A are harmony notes, while the G that connects them is a passing note. Then there are two passing notes in succession, B and C♯, which lead to the next harmony note (D). As you can see, passing notes can come on or off the beat (and are accordingly termed accented or unaccented).

- *Neighbour notes* (N). These are like passing notes, except that they decorate a single harmony note rather than moving between one and another. The D near the end of bar 1, which I mentioned earlier, is an example of this; so is the little E in the top line at the beginning of bar 3. The E and the D after it are played just as if they were both written as eighth notes; the notation makes it obvious that the E is a non-harmony note, but of course not *all* non-harmony notes are notated in this manner.

There is another important kind of non-harmony note, and this is the *suspension*. There are examples of this in bars 37–8 and 39–40 of Example 3, and **Example 6** explains how the second of these works. In (*a*) we have a simple V–I progression. In (*b*) the G in the top line is held over for an extra beat, after the harmony has changed. The result is that there is a *dissonance* at the beginning of the bar: the G no longer fits the harmony. This dissonance is *resolved* on the following beat when the G falls to F. In (*c*) (which is what Bach actually wrote), the B♭ in the right hand is also held over, resulting in a *double suspension*. Though there are no suspensions in bars 1–4 of Example 3, there is one

Ex. 6

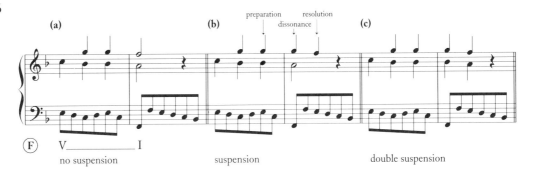

place where a similar thing happens. This is bar 4, where the A and F♯ in the right hand do not belong to the E harmony outlined by the bass. Like a double suspension, these notes fall to G and E, which *are* harmony notes—but by this time, the bass has moved to A. The E minor chord never actually appears, but at the same time it is clearly implied. Hence the II in Example 5.

ASSIGNMENT 1 □

Using the worksheet provided, analyse bars 5–8 and 29–32 of Example 3, modelling the analyses on Example 5 and including the same information. When you have done this, compile a list of the different chord functions (I, V, etc.) in bars 1–8, and the number of times each appears.

If analysing music just meant giving every note a label, then Example 5 would be the last word in analysis. But the point of analysing music is to understand it, and you can't understand music by simply labelling everything in sight, as if you were classifying butterflies or stamps. The problem with music is that you can sense its motions and patterns and symmetries when you listen to it, but when you look at the score all you see is a mass of notes. You see nothing but leaves; the twigs and branches and trunk are hidden. Analysis strips off the details of the musical surface, allowing you to see what lies behind it. Or continuing with the tree analogy, it allows you to see the twigs that support the leaves, and the way the twigs connect with the branches and the branches with the trunk. It reveals the structure that lies behind the immediate effect.

If we want to understand Bach's minuet, then, what is needed is a simplified image of the music that will show the basic framework of its harmony and melody. **Example 7** attempts to provide such a *reduction* for bars 1–4. It picks out the most important harmony notes, which are generally those that coincide with movement in the bass line. That accounts for everything in bars 1 and 4. Bars 2 and 3, however, consist of nothing but tonic harmony; what gives these bars their shape is the rise of the melody from the F♯ at the beginning of bar 2 to the D in bar 3, and its fall to A by the end of that bar. So Example 7 puts in the most important notes of that melodic shape, too—the harmony notes (F♯, A, D, A) and the passing notes that connect them. In addition, it uses slurs to highlight the rising and falling motions that make up the melodic shape. What exactly do these slurs mean? They mean that all of the notes within them belong together. (This is obviously related to the meaning that slurs have in ordinary music; although slurs mean different things in string, wind, and piano scores, all of them indicate that a group of notes belong together.) They also imply that some notes are more important than others; the first slur, for instance, is saying that the F♯ and the D—the

Ex. 7 Reduction of Bach's Op. 5 No. 2, Minuet, bb. 1–4

boundary notes of the group—have an importance that the intervening G, A, B, and C♯ don't. Saying what goes with what, and what is more important than what, is the basis of a great deal of musical analysis, so it's not surprising that analysts make considerable use of slurs. I shall return to this.

What does Example 7 tell us about Bach's music? The answer is, quite a lot. It provides a clear image of the basic melodic shape, or *contour*, that lies behind the detail of the musical surface, and it shows how the contour ties in with the harmonic framework. And this makes it easy to answer the question I asked earlier. The end of bar 4 is a natural break in the music because of two things that happen there. The first is that the wave-like or arch-like contour of the melody throughout bars 1–4 concludes at that point; significantly, there is a leap to the B at the beginning of bar 5. The second is the II–V–I progression—the commonest *cadence* pattern in the whole of Classical music. A cadence is a kind of stopping point, something like a punctuation mark, and we usually define cadences in harmonic terms—so that, for instance, a *perfect* cadence is V–I, while a cadence that ends on V is *imperfect*. (Bar 4 of Example 3 is a perfect cadence.) But not every V–I progression is a cadence. One of the main things that makes *this* V–I a cadence is the way in which it coincides with the melody. Another is the very fact that it comes at the end of the fourth bar; as I said, dance music tends to fall into four-bar sections. Yet another is the trill on the second beat of bar 4; such decoration is commonly found at cadences. None of these things is conclusive in itself. What is conclusive is the way they all work together.

What Example 7 shows is how bars 1–4 make up a single, coherent musical gesture: what we call a *phrase*. And you could make a very similar analysis of the second phrase (that is, bars 5–8), showing how its basic melodic contour rises from B, through C♯ (bar 6), to D, before falling by stages and cadencing on E. The most interesting thing about this phrase is the little decorative arch-like shape in bar 5, moving quickly up to the high B and then falling to the C♯ at the beginning of the bar 6. This little decorative shape isn't part of the basic contour, which as I said goes straight from the B at the beginning of bar 5 to the C♯ in bar 6. But it highlights the movement to the C♯ and D—the highest point of the basic contour. It adds character. If the main contour provides the skeleton of the melody, it is the decoration that fleshes it out and clothes it.

What about the third phrase, bars 9–12? Here we run into a problem, which has to do with the use of Roman letters. Bar 9 consists of a I followed by a VI: so far so good. But the E major chord in bar 10 does not fit; the G♯ is not *diatonic* to D major—that is, it does not belong within the D major scale. What is the G♯ doing there, then? Questions like this are usually best answered by looking ahead to see where the music is going. (It's a paradox that, while you listen to music forwards, you often understand it best by working backwards.) You can see that G♯s remain the norm right up to bar 16. Moreover, there is a cadence on an E major chord in bar 12, and another on an A major chord at bar 16, and the second of these is quite final in its effect—if you stopped playing after the first beat of bar 16, you wouldn't feel that any further chord was immediately implied. Or to put it another way, the A major at bar 16 has taken over the role of tonic for the time being; the music has *modulated* to A major.

This is something that needs to be reflected in a Roman-letter analysis of the passage, as in **Example 8** (where, as you can see, slurs are used to show phrases). The thing *not* to do is to analyse it all in D major; if you do this, as I have shown for bars 9–12, you end up with meaningless progressions such as the V–I–II cadence in bars 11–12. There is no such thing as a V–I–II cadence! If instead you recognize that A major has for the time

Ex. 8 Reduction of
Bach's Op. 5 No. 2,
Minuet, bb. 9–20

being taken over the role of the tonic, and use Roman letters to relate the chords to A instead of D, these bars become a standard cadence on V, and bars 15–16 an equally standard cadence on I; the chord progressions make sense. For purposes of using Roman letters in cases like this, you don't need to know about the intricacies of modulation, which are covered in Chapter 4. A word of warning is in order, however. When you see a note that does not belong to the main key, it doesn't always mean there's a modulation. The D♯ in the bass of bar 11, for instance, does not mean there is a modulation from A major to some other key; it's just a *chromatic* passing note between the D♮ and the E. (That's why it is omitted from the bass line in Example 8.) Again, the C♮ in the right hand at bar 18 does not meant there is a modulation to G major; it's just a splash of G major coloration (and 'coloured', incidentally, is what 'chromatic' literally means). Without going into details at this point, a genuine modulation involves staying in a new key for at least a bar or two, and probably cadencing in it. Anything short of that doesn't need to be reflected in Roman-letter analysis.

On the small scale, chords follow chords; on the large scale, keys follow keys. The scale is different but the principle is similar. All Classical music, and particularly dance music like Bach's Minuet, is constructed like a set of boxes within boxes. Small sections (such as four-bar phrases) are enclosed within larger sections (of perhaps eight or twelve bars), and these larger sections are enclosed within still larger sections. At each level, a section is defined by the key and harmony on which it begins, and that on which it ends. Bars 1–4 begin and end in the tonic, D major; the overall progression of the phrase is *from* I *to* I. That means that it is harmonically *closed*. The second phrase, on the other hand, is harmonically *open*; it moves from IV to V, implying a return to the tonic. This means that the first eight bars as a whole, which are linked together by the double bar line and repeat at the end of bar 8, can be seen as a single open section, moving from I to V. In the same way, bars 9–20 can be seen as a single section again ending on V, and leading to a repeat of the first eight bars—only this time with the cadence altered so that it ends on I. And this means that, at a still larger level, the whole of bars 1–28 can be thought of as a single closed unit, beginning and ending on the tonic. It is as if the music breathed through these rhythmic alternations of opening and closing, which span every level of structure from a single phrase to an entire movement.

Ex. 9 Analysis of
Bach's Op. 5 No. 2,
Minuet, bb. 1–28

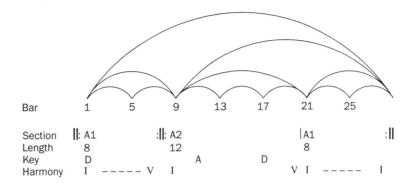

Music can be analysed in words, but charts and diagrams are often more concise and easier to understand. **Example 9** illustrates this by translating most of what I said in the previous paragraph into diagrammatic form. It divides the music into the same main sections (bars 1–8, 9–20, and 21–8) and labels them A¹, A², and A¹ respectively. The sections are called 'A' so as to distinguish them from the contrasted '*Minore*' part of the movement, which would be labelled 'B'; the '1' and '2' are used to show that bars 9–20 are quite different from bars 1–8, whereas bars 21–8 are essentially the same. The next line of Example 9 shows the length of each section in bars, while the following line shows the keys through which the music passes. The bottom line gives the harmonies on which each section begins and ends (and *only* those harmonies), measured of course from the tonic shown on the line above; it shows how two open sections (bars 1–8, 9–20) are followed and concluded by a closed one (bars 21–8).

Finally, and co-ordinated with all of these, there is at the top of the chart a graphic representation of the boxes-within-boxes construction I described. This kind of 'umbrella diagram' is made up of a series of superimposed slurs, with each slur meaning what analytical slurs always mean: a group of notes that belong together, making up a single gesture at some level of musical structure. As you can see, the lowest level of slurs shows the individual phrases; these slurs correspond to the ones in Example 8. The higher-level slurs show the grouping of the phrases into larger units, and the grouping of these units into still larger units.

In this way, Example 9 provides a synopsis of the large-scale design of bars 1–28 of Bach's movement, showing the way its sections balance one another, and providing a context within which to grasp its note-to-note detail. The last clause of that sentence is crucial. People who don't understand musical analysis sometimes attack it for reducing vivid, vibrant works of music to a few meaningless notes or an arid diagram. But analysing music isn't like squeezing an orange to extract the juice, and then throwing away the skin, pith, and seeds. You don't extract the analysis and then throw away the music. Instead, you *return* to the music, using the analysis as a kind of map that shows how everything relates to everything else. The value of the analysis lies in the exploration of the original music that it makes possible. You could say that analytical understanding lies precisely in the gap between Example 9 and the music Bach wrote.

ASSIGNMENT 2 □

Using the worksheet provided, complete the analysis of bars 29–52 of Example 3, modelling it on Example 9, and including the same information. Show only the harmonies on which sections begin or end. (UPPER-CASE keys in the worksheet are major, while lower-case ones are minor.)

Part I

Harmony and Texture

Introduction to Part I

THE subject of Chapter 1 is a musical activity that is sometimes thought to be rather humdrum and of only marginal importance: arrangement. So why begin a study of the Classical style with arrangement?

One reason is that the musicians of the Classical period learned a great deal of their craft through adapting existing music in one way or another. In the 1760s you couldn't hear music at the flick of a switch; public concerts were few and far between, and admission prices were high. If you wanted to hear music, then, you generally had to make it yourself. So people were constantly arranging music for whatever combination of instruments they had available at any one time. If you look in the catalogue of one of the large music libraries, such as the British Library, you will find it crammed with arrangements of Mozart's and Haydn's music for every conceivable instrumental or vocal combination. Arranging Classical music provides an authentic, hands-on experience of it that, at the very least, usefully complements the more theoretical kind of study you can pursue through books.

But there is another, and perhaps better, reason for starting with arrangement. When you transfer music from one instrumental or vocal medium to another, you don't simply work one note at a time. You look *through* the notes on the page to the lines or harmonies that lie behind them. Suppose, for instance, that you are arranging a solo piano piece for strings. In piano writing, the melody or bass line is often hidden within arpeggio patterns; instead of writing the arpeggios into the string parts, you need to extract the melody and bass line, and give the strings those. In this way, you have to decide what is essential in the music, and what is decoration. Equally, you need to decide what goes with what, and where the main breaks are; otherwise you won't know which notes should be given to one instrument and which to another, or where to change the pattern of instrumentation. And these are basic *analytical* decisions. Arranging music, then, is a form of analysis; it develops theoretical concepts in a practical context.

Much the same applies to accompaniment. This, again, was one of the practical activities through which Classical musicians learned their craft; as Chapter 2 shows, they were expected to be able to 'realize' a bass line by filling out the required harmonies. (Although this is something we associate mainly with the Baroque, it was a skill that musicians retained right through the Classical period.) And just as you need an analytical grasp of music to arrange it, so you need to understand the harmonic implications of a bass line in order to fill it out in this way. You need to grasp its phrase structure and cadential organization: good accompaniment, like good performance, renders the music articulate by bringing out these things. Like arrangement, then, accompaniment is a practical activity that depends on, and at the same time fosters, a theoretical understanding of music.

At first sight, both arrangement and accompaniment are concerned primarily with texture, that is to say the sonorous fabric in which tunes and chords are clothed. And to that extent, this section focuses on texture. At a deeper level, however, the focus is on harmony. Sometimes defined as the art or science of combining sounds, harmony is much more than that. It deals not just with simultaneities—with what happens at any one point in time—but with what happens *through* time. It is harmony that is ultimately responsible for the sense of purposeful motion and logical patterning that characterizes the music of J. C. Bach, Haydn, Mozart, and Beethoven. In this way, texture is the outer fabric, but harmony goes to the heart of the Classical sound.

Further reading

- Between them, Chapter 1 and Appendix 2 provide all you really need to know about instrumentation at this stage. Further details are however available in a number of texts, such as Samuel Adler, *The Study of Orchestration* (New York, 1982).
- A fuller treatment of figured bass and associated accompaniment techniques, along with a brief but systematic outline of common-practice harmony, may be found in a number of keyboard harmony texts such as Allen Brings *et al.*, *A New Approach to Keyboard Harmony* (New York, 1979). Classical music is largely keyboard-orientated; a good foundation in keyboard harmony forms the best possible starting point for studying the Classical style.
- Mozart's concertos based on J. C. Bach's sonatas are not widely known, but may be found in the standard complete edition of Mozart's works, the *Neue Mozart-Ausgabe* (x/28/2). Edwin J. Simon surveyed them in his article 'Sonata into Concerto: A Study of Mozart's First Seven Concertos', *Acta Musicologica*, 21 (1959), 170–85.
- For a more detailed discussion of the role of analysis in arrangement, see my article 'Arrangement as Analysis', *Journal of Music Theory Pedagogy*, 1 (1987), 77–89.

CHAPTER 1

Arrangement

Ex. 10 Haydn, Divertimento in C, Hob. XIV: 10, Minuet. Reproduced from *J. Haydn: Werke*, Vol. XVI by permission of G. Henle Verlag, München

IN 1760, two years before J. C. Bach took up residence in London, Joseph Haydn began his long period of service as Kapellmeister (or Master of Music) for the aristocratic Esterházy family in what is now Austria, but was at that time part of the Austro-Hungarian empire. As Kapellmeister, Haydn's job was not just to organize music in the Esterházy's private chapel (as the title implies), but to provide music for any number of social occasions. Some of the music was no doubt intended for performance by members of the Esterházy family and their friends, and Haydn wrote a good deal of technically undemanding music during these years. A combination that was particularly popular among amateurs was keyboard (harpsichord or piano) plus one, two, or three

Menuet

stringed instruments. **Example 10** shows the minuet movement of a little divertimento which Haydn wrote some time during the 1760s. As you can see, all that survives is a keyboard part, but the original manuscript has 'con Violini' written on it. The music was almost certainly intended to be played by one of the commonest combinations, keyboard plus two violins and a cello.

What would these missing parts have been like? Of course there is no way of knowing *exactly* how they went. But if you look at other examples of this sort of music, in which the string parts do survive, you can make a pretty good guess. **Examples 11** and **12** show the first half of two minuets that date from around the same time as Example 10 (though there are some doubts as to whether Example 11 is actually by Haydn). You can see that there is a basic formula for this combination of instruments: the first violin doubles the top line of the keyboard part most of the time, the bass doubles the bottom line of the keyboard part almost all the time, and the second violin fills in the **texture** as best it can.

This means that adding the first violin and cello to Example 10 is easy. In fact you could simply copy out their parts from the keyboard part. But you would have to do it in pencil, and then use a eraser: in both Examples 11 and 12, the first violin and cello parts sometimes omit notes so as to lighten the texture or add rhythmic interest. However, copying out parts in this mechanical manner isn't the best way to set about arranging

Ex. 11 Haydn, Divertimento in C, Hob. XIV: C2, Minuet

Ex. 12 Haydn, Divertimento in C, Hob. XIV: 8, Minuet

Menuet

music. Instead, you should start by really getting to know the music, rather as if you were rehearsing it for a performance. (A Roman-letter analysis might be a useful part of this.) Then, when you come to arrange the music, you will be able to write parts that express your understanding of it. In this way, arranging music involves interpretation just as much as performance does.

It's harder to know what to do with the second violin, because there is no simple rule for it. But we can draw up a list of possibilities by looking at Examples 11 and 12. The second violin can:

- Double the inner line of the keyboard part, if there is one. (This is all that happens in Example 11 until the last two bars.)
- Move in *parallel* thirds or sixths (occasionally tenths) with the first violin, providing of course that this makes sense in harmonic terms.
- Less often, move in parallel thirds or sixths with the cello—again providing this makes harmonic sense.
- Fill in missing notes of the harmony. This is a particularly good thing to do when

the other parts don't include the third of the chord: thirds create a sense of harmonic fullness, and Classical composers rarely left them out except when they were writing in unison or octaves as a special effect. This use of the second violin isn't found in either Example 11 or 12, but there is something like it in bar 9 of **Example 13**. This is from a divertimento (again maybe by Haydn, maybe not) in which there is only one violin; as you can see, the role of the violin is basically the same as that of the second violin in the divertimenti for two violins and bass.

- Sustain a ***pedal note***, that is a note that is shared by a succession of harmonies. Again Example 13 illustrates this. The effect is to bind the chord progression together and create continuity; you can often hear the horns playing pedal notes in Classical symphonies.

Ex. 13 Haydn, Divertimento in C, Hob. XIV: C1, Minuet

Menuet

Before you try the first assignment, you need to know about a number of conventions of Classical ***part-writing***. Textbooks generally express these conventions in the form of rules or prohibitions, as follows (**Example 14**):

- No parallel fifths or octaves
- Leading notes rise
- Sevenths fall
- No doubled leading notes, sevenths, or thirds

But it's not correct to think of these as if they were traffic regulations: music isn't like that. Rather, they indicate what *normally* happens. Parallel fifths and octaves destroy the

Ex. 14

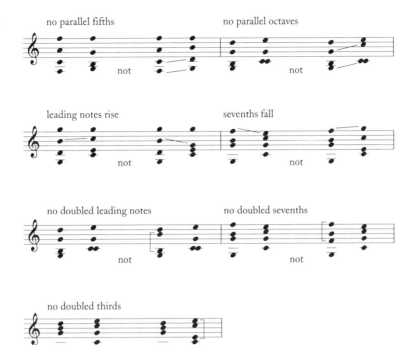

sense that the parts are independent from each other; it is as if two parts had collapsed into one. Now Classical composers in general liked to maintain a kind of equilibrium between the different parts. So they *normally* avoided parallel fifths and octaves. As for leading notes and sevenths, it's hard to say just *why* these rise and fall respectively, but they have a natural tendency to do so, and you get a feeling of discontinuity if they don't. Classical composers in general aimed at continuity, and so they *normally* respected these tendencies. And given this, it's obvious why they avoided doubling leading notes and sevenths, because if they had doubled them, then *either* the leading notes and sevenths would have had to move the wrong way, *or* they would have ended up with parallel octaves. As for thirds, these seem to call too much attention to themselves if they are doubled, again disturbing the textural balance of the music.

But none of these so-called 'rules' are rigid. Whenever there was a good reason to break them (for instance, so as to write a well-shaped instrumental part), Classical composers were ready and willing to do so. This particularly applies where inner parts are concerned, since these are not as prominent as the outer ones. And in keyboard or orchestral writing, of course, it's standard procedure to double the same line in different octaves.

ASSIGNMENT 3 □

Add two violin parts and a cello part to Example 10. Begin by completing the Roman-letter analysis in the worksheet. Then write the first violin and cello parts, and finally add the second violin. Model your style on Examples 11, 12, and 13, and refer to them when you need guidance, but do not follow them slavishly. Your aim should be to write a piece of plausible and playable music in a more or less Haydnesque style, not to cobble together a series of extracts from Haydn's compositions. Appendix 2 provides guidance on instrumental ranges.

London was one of the most lucrative stops on the international touring circuit, and for that reason Leopold Mozart took his prodigy son there during 1764–5. The 8-year-old Wolfgang performed, composed, and generally made a hit with the same fashionable classes who were purchasing J. C. Bach's Op. 5 a year or two later. While in London, Mozart studied with Bach, and Bach's music became one of the main influences on his own compositional style. Some time after this encounter, Mozart turned several of Bach's keyboard sonatas into small-scale concertos for his own use. To do this, he interpolated orchestral sections of his own, or simply added strings to what Bach had written. **Example 15** is Mozart's arrangement of bars 29–52 from the Minuet I discussed in the Introduction (Op. 5 No. 2; I have renumbered the bars so that they correspond to Example 3.) As you can see, Mozart left the keyboard part exactly as Bach wrote it, merely adding two violins and a cello, and so ending up with the same instrumental group as in Haydn's divertimenti.

Sometimes Mozart used the instruments in the same way as Haydn did: the cello generally doubles the lowest line of the keyboard part (though with a few octave *transpositions*), and in bars 33–4 the first violin doubles the top line of the keyboard part, while the second violin fills in the harmony. But Mozart doesn't stick as closely to the formula as Haydn. In bars 29–33 he gives chords to the strings that don't appear in Bach's original, providing rhythmic emphasis and bringing out the two-bar pattern of the melodic *sequence*. In bars 38–41 he again brings out the sequence, this time by means of a three-note violin figure that answers the keyboard part. And from bars 41–4, where the music turns towards G minor, the strings are silent, coming in again when the opening idea returns. Each of these examples shows how Mozart is not just arranging the music mechanically, one note at a time. Instead, he is *interpreting* Bach's music, and composing his interpretation into the score.

The following assignment involves arranging the corresponding passage from a Bach sonata that Mozart didn't turn into a concerto: Op. 5 No. 1 (**Example 16**). There are a number of ways in which this passage is different from the one in Op. 5 No. 2. The main difference is that it isn't a closed section: it ends on V, leading up to the return of the opening idea. In fact the whole middle section is really a long *dominant preparation*. Although it begins with alternations of forte and piano, there is a crescendo marking at bar 39, which effectively lasts up to the end of the section. This needs to be composed into your arrangement. Because of this, you probably won't want to use pizzicato strings, as Mozart did (that was his way of composing Bach's piano marking into the music). You will also need to find accompaniment figures for the strings that reinforce the forte/piano alternations at the beginning of the section, and the crescendo at the end of it.

ASSIGNMENT 4

Arrange Example 16 for keyboard, first and second violins, and cello. The F in the left hand during the first eight bars is a pedal note; as the Roman-letter analysis shows, it sometimes contradicts the harmony above it. (The notation V^7/V means 'V^7 of V'; the harmony is C^7—a dominant seventh with C as its root—plus the F pedal.) **Example 17** *clarifies the harmony in bars 37–40; try to avoid writing parallel fifths at this point.*

Ex. 15 Mozart, Concerto after J. C. Bach, KV 107, Minuet

Ex. 15 *cont.*

Da capo Tempo di Menuetto al Fine

Ex. 16 J. C. Bach, Sonata Op. 5 No. 1, Minuet, bb. 29–46

Ex. 17

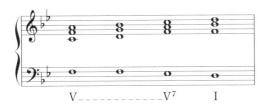

In the years around 1770, Mozart, now in his teens, wrote dozens of orchestral dances, mainly minuets and trios. **Example 18** shows one of them. As you can see, the core of the little orchestra is the strings. But in the minuet (not the trio) they are supplemented by oboes and trumpets (these are small trumpets in D, called *clarini*, sounding a major second above the written part). I say 'supplemented' because while the oboes and trumpets add colour and emphasis, the string parts would make perfectly good sense played by themselves. Somebody (not Mozart) arranged these dances for keyboard, and **Example 19** shows the arrangement of Example 18. **Example 20** is the keyboard version of another minuet and trio, dating from about 1770, but in this case the orchestral version has been lost (though Mozart reused the Trio in another set of dances written a year or two later). The third project in this chapter is to orchestrate Example 20. And the best way to approach this is through a careful comparison of Examples 18 and 19.

It immediately becomes obvious that the keyboard version isn't a literal, note-for-note transcription of the orchestral one; compare the bass line in bars 2–3 as it appears in the two versions. Again, the keyboard version misses out the A pedal in bars 5–8; a two-part texture consisting mainly of tenths sounds perfectly good on the piano, but it would leave a hole in the texture if transcribed directly for string orchestra (unless there was a harpsichord continuo to fill in the gap, of course). So one of your main concerns will be inventing string figures that fill out the keyboard texture. The second violin part in Mozart's Trio is a good example of this: it has a moving line that matches the eighth-note pattern of the melody, in place of the chords in the left hand of the keyboard version.

If you use a similar figuration for the trio of Example 20, you may find yourself wondering what chords to use on the eighth notes. This is a non-problem: the harmony changes at most every quarter note, and sometimes more slowly. For comparison, look at the first bar of the Trio in Example 18, where there is only one harmony, D major. The first violin plays a passing note (the E) and a neighbour note (the C#); the C# is actually on the beat. But that doesn't give it any harmonic significance in its own right. It would be quite incorrect to put it together with the other parts and read a D^7 chord on the third beat of the bar. In the same way, there aren't F# minor chords on the third beat of bar 4 (the bass line is simply *en route* from A to D) or the second eighth note of bar 6, where the violins' F#s are passing notes. There is a general point to be made here. Many Classical musical textures consist of a relatively slow harmonic motion elaborated by faster-moving figuration. Trying to create real harmonic motions at the level of the smallest notes would produce a clogged effect, something like a Bach chorale harmonization being played much too fast.

It's easiest to write the string parts first and then add the winds. They correspond to the dynamic markings in Example 19—'forte' means the winds play; 'piano' means they don't. But there aren't dynamic markings in Example 20 (except in the Trio). So you will have to make up your own mind. But there is a general principle: everyone plays at the beginning and at the cadences. Writing for oboes is quite straightfoward, and you'll see

Ex. 18 Mozart, Twelve Minuets, No. 3, KV 103

Trio

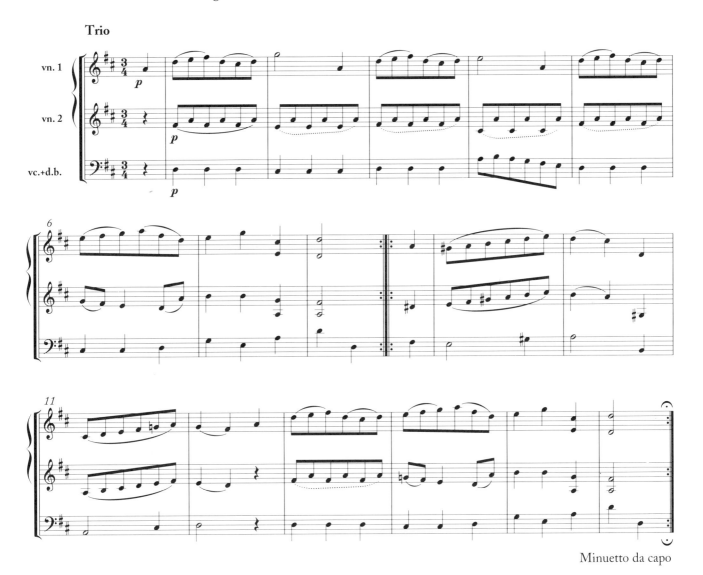

Minuetto da capo

that they generally double the strings (but sometimes at a different octave). Trumpets, however, are more specialized. In the Classical era, neither trumpets nor horns had valves; as a result, they could produce only a limited range of notes. **Example 21** shows the notes available (or at least those that were commonly used), together with some typical patterns for two-part writing. Players used different crooks to transpose these notes to the tonic of the piece they were playing—hence the trumpets in D of Example 18. You can see why Classical composers used these instruments primarily to outline dominant–tonic progressions, providing punctuation and highlighting the music's phrase structure.

A final point: Mozart sometimes uses *double* or ***triple stops*** in the violins to add emphasis, particularly at cadences. (You may have also noticed them in Example 15.) If you are not a string player, you may prefer not to use them. If you do use them, here are some guidelines:

• It's easiest to play double or triple stops when one or more of the notes are on open strings. This is the only way in which you can play two notes more than an octave apart (as in bars 20–21 of the minuet in Example 18, first violins).

Ex. 19 Mozart, Twelve Minuets, No. 3, arrangement

Menuetto da capo

Ex. 20 Mozart, Minuet in C, KV 61^g II, arrangement

Menuetto

Trio

(d)   V^7_____ I   (C)   V^7____

I _____ V   Minuetto da capo

Ex. 21

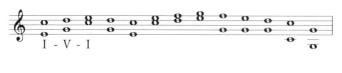

I - V - I

V - I of V

- Because of the slant of the left hand, it's more comfortable to play fifths, sixths and sevenths than thirds or fourths. That's why you often find interlocking double stops between first and second violins (see bars 7–8 of the Trio).
- It's possible to play triple-stopped triads, but only if there's an interval of a sixth or more between the outer notes (see bar 10 of the Minuet).

ASSIGNMENT 5

Arrange Example 20 for an orchestra consisting of 2 oboes, 2 clarini in C (sounding at written pitch), first and second violins, and celli doubled by double basses. Write the string parts first and then add the winds. Remember that, unlike in Assignments 3 and 4, there is no keyboard part and therefore the instrumental parts must be complete and self-sufficient. Here are some notes to help you:

- *Minuet, bars 1–2: the Gs are pedal notes; you don't have to fit each of them into a triadic harmony. But you need to fill out the texture. (By analogy, you could add C pedals in bars 3–4.)*
- *Minuet, bars 9–15: beware of simply transcribing the left hand as a cello part.*
- *Trio: what are you going to do about the dynamic markings? Although it's not idiomatic to use brass instruments in trios like this, Mozart might well have included the oboes.*
- *Trio, bars 9–12: The harmony is slightly complex and I have added a Roman-letter analysis. (Remember that 'd'—lower-case D—means D minor.)*

ASSIGNMENT 6

The previous assignments have kept to the instrumental combinations used by Classical composers, in an attempt to achieve some kind of historical authenticity. But Classical composers frequently arranged their music for whatever instruments they had at hand on a particular occasion. Following the spirit rather than the letter of Classical music, arrange either Example 19 or Example 20 for whatever contemporary instruments you have available (saxophones, vibraphones, electronic keyboards, etc.).

CHAPTER 2

Accompaniment

THE 1770s and 1780s were the golden age of Freemasonry in Vienna, and many of the most famous composers of the day belonged to this supposedly secret society. Among them was Mozart, and **Example 22** shows the manuscript of a song he composed in 1772 for use in lodge meetings. The text is a celebration of the joys of brotherhood (the Freemasons were an all-male society), and you can see from the transcription in **Example 23** that a chorus comes in at the end. You can also see that the song is written in just two parts: voice—tenor, of course, not soprano—and bass line. Mozart has adopted the not-quite-extinct Baroque practice of writing only a left hand part for the keyboard player, who is expected to fill out the chords with his (and I do mean his) right hand. Mozart gives no indication of the harmony that is required: the performer has to work this out on the basis of what *is* written, as well as finding an appropriate texture for the accompaniment. To use the normal term for it, he has to 'realize' Mozart's score. And to provide some guidance as to what such a realization might look like, **Example 24** shows a typical modern edition of another song, in praise of Joy, that Mozart wrote a few years earlier; again, Mozart wrote only the melody and the bass line, so that everything in the right hand part of the accompaniment has been added by the editor.

We can make some general observations. The right hand more or less follows the melody, but in a simplified form: it doesn't leap about the keyboard, following the vocal line, but as far as possible keeps in the same place. When the right hand has a three-note chord, this can be in *close position* (as in bars 19–24) or in *open position*, omitting whatever note is in the bass. Often there are only two notes in the right hand, giving a complete triadic harmony together with the bass. But the accompaniment doesn't have

Ex. 22 Mozart, *Lobgesang auf die feier-liche Johannisloge*, KV 148, autograph

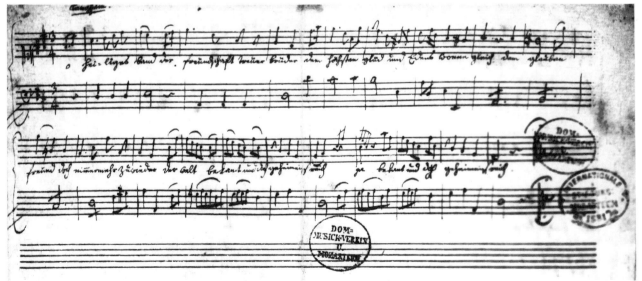

Ex. 23 Mozart, *Lobgesang auf die feierliche Johannisloge*

to include all the notes of the triad: for instance, the F chord in bar 3 is missing its fifth. Nor is there a chord on every beat. In fact the most important thing in doing this kind of realization is to know when the real harmony changes are, so that you can bring them out in your accompaniment. What you want to avoid is clogging up the texture by playing a chord whenever there's a little bit of melodic motion.

So, for instance, there's no reason to play more than one chord in each of the first two bars. You *could* add B♮–C in the right hand on the second beat of bar 2, so creating a new chord there (a VII of C, to be precise), but it would be fussy and unnecessary. In each of these bars the bass line is much better seen as just a passing-note motion from the third to the root of the harmony, and the editor underlines this by adding an inner line that moves from the fifth to the third. In bars 3–4, on the other hand, the editor treats each of the notes in the bass as a harmony note, completing the triads in the right hand, because they form an approach to the cadence (which, incidentally, is a V–VI or **interrupted** cadence). The result is that the chord changes start slowly and speed up towards the cadence. In this way the accompaniment brings out the harmonic rhythm that is implied in Mozart's melody and bass line; it heightens the impression that bars 1–4 make up a single, coherent musical phrase. To this extent, it represents an interpretation of Mozart's music, rather than a mechanical completion of the notes.

Like most keyboard music, the editor's accompaniment is sometimes **homophonic**, consisting of a series of chords, and sometimes **contrapuntal**, consisting of a number of superimposed lines. And again like most keyboard music, the one texture merges imperceptibly into the other. For instance, in the first two bars, the right hand clearly consists of two lines. Bars 3–4 consist of a series of chords, but they are consistently in three parts;

Ex. 24 Mozart, *An die Freude*, KV 53 (with realization of bass)

Ex. 24 *cont.*

Hö - re mich von dei - nem Thro - ne, Kind der Weis - heit, de - ren Hand im - mer selbst in dei - ne Kro - ne ih - re schön - sten Ro - sen band, ih - re schön - sten Ro - sen band!

you could easily transcribe these bars, and the next, for string trio. (The editor's rather fussy notation even suggests that there are two lines playing a single note, F, in bar 5.) But in bar 6 there's suddenly another part, which disappears in bar 7. Then it reappears in bars 11–12. Really, of course, there aren't parts at all at these points. It's just a question of chords being thickened at cadence points. So there is no need to keep to a fixed number of parts throughout when realizing a keyboard part like this. In fact it would be downright unidiomatic to do so.

How far do the conventions of Classical part-writing (as set out in the previous chapter) apply to this style of keyboard accompaniment? They certainly apply to the top notes in the right hand, because these are quite prominent. Here, then, you should generally avoid things like parallel fifths or octaves with the bass. When it comes to the inner notes it's not so important, because nobody is likely to hear them as separate parts.

ASSIGNMENT 7 □

This assignment is in three parts.

- *Make an analysis of Example 24. Begin by adding slurs above the music to indicate the phrases (the first slur is shown). Then identify the keys through which the music passes, writing them in the circles. Finally add Roman letters, but only when there is a real change of harmony, omitting passing formations. (Use the notation VII°⁷ for the **diminished seventh chords** in bars 21 and 23.)*

- *List the chord functions you have found, and the number of times each appears.*

- *Classify each cadence as perfect, imperfect, or interrupted.*

As I said, neither of the songs in Examples 23 and 24 contains any indication of the harmonies: you have to work them out for yourself. But Mozart, like other Classical composers, sometimes used a shorthand system for indicating harmonies, and this is *figured bass*. It is a shorthand system in the sense that you don't write out all the notes in the accompaniment—you just write the bass line, and add figures that show the notes to be played above it. Fluency in interpreting these figures was an essential part of a keyboard player's competence in the Baroque and early Classical era. As an illustration, **Example 25** adds figures (mine, not Mozart's) to the bass line from the first twelve bars of Example 24. The harmonic interpretation shown is the same as the editor's, so you can match up the figures in Example 25 with the right hand part in Example 24 to see how the system works.

The basic principles are simple:

- The figures tell you to play the note a given interval above the bass. For instance, the ⁶ above the first note in Example 25 means that you should add the note a sixth above the bass, that is F, while the ³ means that you should add a C. (The system doesn't specify register, so you could equally well play the C a tenth above the bass.)

- It's a matter of simple arithmetic to work out that a note figured ⁵₃ will represent a root position triad, while ⁶₃ will represent a first inversion triad, and ⁶₄ a second inversion triad. However, you rarely see the first two of these, because of a system of

Ex. 25

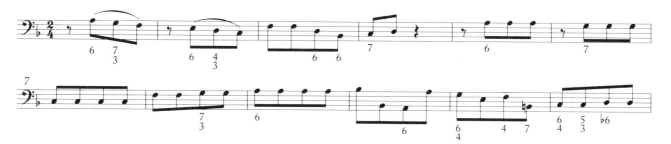

abbreviations. If you just see ^{6}, you assume that $^6_3$ is intended; if you see no figures at all, you assume that $^5_3$ is intended. (Given this, you may be able to see why I put a ^{6} below the E in bar 2 of Example 25, even though there isn't a C in the editor's realization.) The point of this is to cut down the number of figures you have to read or write.

ASSIGNMENT 8 □

Figure the bass of bars 13–40 of Example 24. Your figures should correspond to the editor's realization.

ASSIGNMENT 9 □

Example 26 *shows Laat ons juichen, a song of praise written for the installation of Prince William of Orange by the little-known composer Christian Graaf; Mozart wrote a set of keyboard variations on it in 1766 (KV 24), when he was nine years old. Continue the realization of the figured bass in the worksheet. (The dashes after the figures in bars 10–11 mean that the harmony doesn't change. Don't attempt to harmonize the sixteenth notes in bar 12 separately, either.) Here are some notes to help you:*

- *Keep to the format of the bass line in the left hand and between one and three notes in the right, with the right hand moving as little as possible (except between phrases). The aim is to provide the minimum necessary backing for the voice, not to write a keyboard solo.*

- *Similarly, don't try to echo every little detail of the melody in your accompaniment, or worry about minor clashes between them. Bear in mind that this is a harpsichord-based style, and that the harpsichord is a percussive instrument; full chords, in particular, should be used to bring out harmonic changes and to outline cadences. When you play is almost more important than what you play.*

This and the following assignment are best done at the keyboard. (If you can sing the vocal part while you play, so much the better.)

ASSIGNMENT 10 □

Continue the realization of Example 23 shown in the worksheet. Here are some notes to help you:

- *Begin by observing key changes, identifying inessential notes, and deciding what the implied harmonies are. If you do this correctly, writing in the notes should be quite straightforward.*

- *The only chords required in this setting are I, II, V (including V⁷), and VI (all related, of course, to the current tonic). Bear in mind that these chords may occur in any inversion, including third inversion in the case of V⁷ (that is, with the seventh in the bass).*

- *Bars 9–10: this is a Mozart cliché. Bar 9 has to be understood in relation to A major, bar 10 in relation to D. The right hand of the accompaniment should follow the implied A–G#–G♮–F# line.*

- *Bars 13–14, 17–18: the melody on the first two beats of these bars contains accented passing notes—passing notes that come on the beats, with the harmony notes on the off-beats.*

Ex. 26 Christian
Graaf, *Laat ons juichen*

- Other, more exotic, combinations of figures result from other chords—for example, seventh chords in their various inversions—or from passing notes (as in the first two bars of Example 25). Remember that the figures don't necessarily relate to *chords* as such: they simply say what notes are to be played above the bass line.

- The system works in terms of the key signature currently in use. But you can show chromatic notes by adding accidentals after the figures, as in bar 12 of Example 25. If you see just an accidental, without a figure, this is another abbreviation: it refers to the third above the bass.

It's important to have some knowledge of some figured bass, partly so that you can interpret the music for yourself instead of relying on a editor, and partly because terminology derived from it is widely used today in analysing music. Its particular value is that, unlike Roman letters, it leads you to think of harmonic progressions in terms of the actual notes in the bass line. Although its use as a performance device was well into decline in Mozart's lifetime—composers generally wanted to write out their music in full, rather than giving the performer a shorthand notation—it continued throughout the Classical period as a way of *thinking* music. Mozart used figured bass when he taught composition. And you can even see the occasional figured bass line in Beethoven's sketches.

The little song in **Example 27**, *Das Kinderspiel* or 'Children's play', dates from the last year of Mozart's life, but it could hardly be more simple and artless. (Or at least that is the impression it makes, though the text contains a sting in the tail which evidently appealed to Mozart's sometimes macabre sense of humour.) It is much more intimate than the songs in Examples 23 and 24, and seems better suited for domestic performance—not least because its textures are clearly intended for piano rather than harpsichord. The right hand of the piano part doubles the voice, while the left hand adds a bass line with a broken chord pattern above it. Because of the prevailing sixteenth-note motion of both the voice and the piano part, there are a lot of notes on the page—and yet the effect is light and uncluttered, because the music is built on a very simple harmonic plan. The best way to grasp this plan is by sitting at the keyboard and playing the same kind of simplified accompaniment you were writing in Assignment 10. **Example 28** shows what I mean. It picks out the notes that are most important harmonically, and so presents the basic structure that lies behind all the little notes of Mozart's song. (You will see that I have used barlines to separate out its different phrases.)

Example 28 makes it obvious just how very simple the song's harmonic structure is. There is only one chord in each bar. And these chords consist of I, II, IV, and V—and that is all, apart from the III in bar 13. Even this III is hardly a chord in its own right; it is just part of a series of first inversion chords connecting the IV at the beginning of bar 13 with the V at bar 15. **Example 29** clarifies this connection. Here the rhythmic aspect of the music is not important, and that is why I have used just note-heads.

Expressed in terms of Roman letters, then, Mozart uses only *four* real harmonic functions! But here we come to one of the limitations of Roman letters. As far as Roman letters are concerned, it makes no difference what note is in the bass, as long as it belongs to the chord in question. So **Example 30** would result in exactly the same Roman-letter analysis as the first five bars of what Mozart wrote. Musically, however, it's much less successful. The difference is that, in Example 30, all the chords are in root position, whereas Mozart makes free use of different inversions: first inversion in bars 3, 5 and 6, and second inversion in bar 2. This allows Mozart to keep the bass moving when the harmony remains the same across two bars (bars 2–3 and 4–5), while the C♯ in the bass at bar 5 drives through D and E to the cadence in bar 8 in a way that the A of Example 30 does not. By comparison to Mozart's version, Example 30 is utterly pedestrian, not to say flat-footed. (It also creates parallel fifths in the left hand at bars 5–6, and gets the hands tangled with one another.)

We can summarize the use of inversions as follows:

- They enable you to design bass lines that have a distinctive contour and a sense of going somewhere.

- They allow you to sustain a sense of movement even when the harmony doesn't change.

- They create a lighter effect than a series of root position chords. For instance, a V–I cadence with the I in first inversion sounds less final than when the I is in root position.

Ex. 27 Mozart, *Das Kinderspiel*, KV 598

Ex. 28

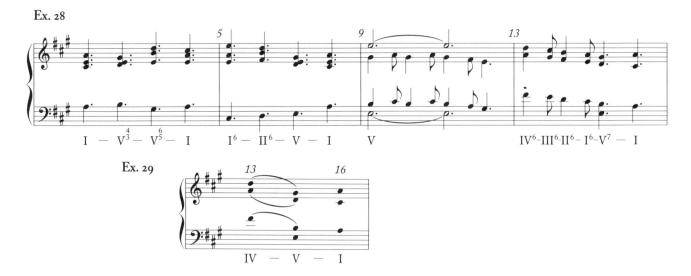

Ex. 29

- First inversions are essential whenever you have a series of chords moving in parallel, as in bars 13–14 of *Das Kinderspiel*. If they were in root position you would end up with a series of parallel fifths.

- They are particularly useful in cadences. I in first inversion is an effective launching pad for a IV-V–I cadence, or a II–V–I cadence if the II is also in first inversion (as in Example 28, bars 5–8)

- I in second inversion also has a special role in cadences, which you can see in bar 15 of Example 24: the C and E fall to B and D, giving a V chord. This—the so-called cadential six-four—one of the very few ways in which second inversion chords are

Ex. 30

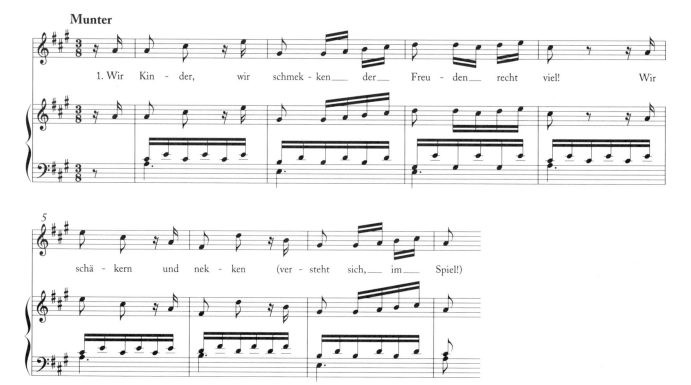

used in Classical music. In fact, because it serves purely as an approach to the V, it is really better to think of the second inversion I as not a chord in its own right, but just a V with two passing notes or *appoggiaturas*.

Because inversion plays such an important role in harmonic structure, it's useful to have a notation for it. One system is to add letters after the Roman letter to show the inversion, so that I^b means a first inversion tonic, I^c a second inversion one, and so forth. Nowadays, however, it's more usual to use a combination of Roman letters and figured bass notation. You can see these figures in Example 28. The meaning of the figures remains the same as in figured bass: ^{6} means first inversion, $^6_4$ means second inversion, and so on. There are a couple of complications with this notation, however. One is that it contradicts the common practice of using V^7 to refer to a dominant seventh chord *in any inversion*: according to the system I have just explained, a dominant seventh chord in first inversion ought to be V^6_5, but in practice it is often referred to simply as V^7. The other has to do with the second inversion I, to which I referred in the previous paragraph. You would expect it to be called a I^6_4, giving rise to a I^6_4-V progression, and some people do indeed call it that. But many musicians prefer to refer to it as a V^{6-5}_{4-3} because this makes it clear that the I^6_4 isn't really a chord in its own right.

ASSIGNMENT 11 □

The worksheet shows 'Sophie's song' from an opera performed in Vienna around 1778; it is by another little known composer, Ignaz Umlauf, and tells of the relief from sorrow that hope can bring. Complete the piano accompaniment shown. No postlude is necessary. Here are some notes to help you:

- *You need use nothing but I, II, and V chords. The skill lies in choosing the right inversions to produce a well-shaped bass line. You will need to use first inversions freely; the only second inversion chord you should use is V^6_4 (a.k.a. I^6_4, see above).*

- *The arpeggio patterns are regular and easy to write once you know what the chords are. So the best approach is to work out a simple chordal accompaniment along the lines of Example 28, and then add the arpeggio patterns at the end. There is no need to worry about small dissonances between the voice and the piano: they add spice to the music.*

Part II

Harmony and Line

Introduction to Part II

THE relationship between harmony and line is one of the hardest things to explain in the whole of Classical music. It's rather like explaining how to ride a bicycle: the individual components are easy enough to explain (you pedal with your feet, you turn the handlebars in the direction you want to go, and so on), but the difficulty lies in doing all these things at the same time. In the same way, you can't write a tune in the Classical style, or add a bass line to an existing tune, without at the same time being aware of its harmonic implications; but equally, you can't work out the harmony without thinking of the way the lines should go—particularly the bass line, which is the foundation of Classical harmony. Or is harmony the foundation of the Classical bass line? Both seem equally true; the truth is that you can't think about either harmony or bass lines in isolation. Each depends on the other, and so you have to conceive or understand them together.

Both harmony and line, however, are subject to what might be called the law of the cadence. One of the essential characteristics of Classical music is that it is punctuated by frequent cadences—temporary stopping places, points of articulation where the threads of the musical fabric come together into a kind of knot. Cadences define phrases, and both harmony and line are shaped within the controlling context of the phrase. Melodies are shaped into expressive contours that usually rise to a central point and then fall to the cadence (the word 'cadence' literally means 'fall'). Harmonic progressions gain their shape through moving from a starting point to a destination point or goal—and this is again the cadence. This means that you don't understand Classical music by beginning at the beginning and working through it until you get to the end; you understand it by identifying the phrases into which it falls, and seeing how harmony and line are designed to create a sense of continuous, purposeful motion within the context of each phrase. (At a more abstract level of analysis you can do much the same for larger musical sections.)

A good deal of this section deals with miniature dances consisting of a melody and a bass line, and made up of four phrases each of four bars. Such dances exhibit the essential characteristics of the Classical style in the most concise form possible. And for this reason they were extensively used in the Classical period as a means of introducing the basic principles of music. Chapters 3 and 4 are drawn in part from Heinrich Koch's *Introductory Essay on Composition*, written in the 1780s, and at various points I cite other teachers and theorists of the period, such as Francesco Galeazzi and Joseph Riepel. These names were little known until 1979, when Leonard Ratner published his *Classic Music: Expression, Form, and Style*. In this book Ratner outlined an essentially new approach to the understanding of Classical music. Instead of simply studying the scores, he tried to reconstruct the way in which people *thought* about music during the Classical era. Composition manuals and theoretical treatises naturally formed one of his chief sources, and his book remains the indispensable introduction to the world of Classical music as the musicians of the time saw it.

Composition manuals tell us quite a lot. But there is a more direct way of finding out how people learned to compose in the eighteenth century, and that is by looking at their workbooks. Composition was taught through private lessons, and many of the major composers of the time had pupils. And in a few cases, such as that of Mozart's pupil Thomas Attwood, the workbooks they used have survived to the present day. As a result, we can see the kind of curriculum Mozart planned out for Attwood, and the assignments he set; we can even see his corrections of Attwood's work, and try to figure out why Mozart thought what Attwood did was good or bad. That is the topic of Chapter 5.

Further reading

- A substantial portion of Heinrich Koch's composition manual is available in an English translation by Nancy Kovaleff Baker under the title *Introductory Essay on Composition: The Mechanical Rules of Melody, Sections 3 and 4* (New Haven, 1983).
- Leonard Ratner, *Classic Music: Expression, Form, and Style* (New York, 1979). The indispensable source for the study of the period theoretical background of Classical music. The quotation from Francesco Galeazzi in Chapter 3 is taken from Ratner's 'Ars Combinatoria' in H. C. Robbins Landon and Roger Chapman (eds.), *Studies in Eighteenth-Century Music* (London, 1970), 348.
- My account of Attwood's studies with Mozart is based in part on Daniel Heartz's article 'Thomas Attwood's Lessons in Composition with Mozart', *Proceedings of the Royal Musical Association*, 100 (1973–4), 175–83. The Attwood notebook is published as part of the *Neue Mozart-Ausgabe* (x/30/1). A more comprehensive survey of the great composers as teachers, in the form of a series of case studies, is William Mann's *Theory and Practice: The Great Composer as Student and Teacher* (New York, 1987).
- A good keyboard harmony manual (such as *A New Approach to Keyboard Harmony*, mentioned in the Introduction to Part I) remains valuable as a background to this section. Diatonic and chromatic sequence patterns, in particular, are useful as a repertory of harmonic progressions for fitting into any given compositional context.

CHAPTER 3

Melody and bass

HEINRICH KOCH, who wrote the little minuet shown in **Example 31,** was in many ways the typical late eighteenth-century German musician. Like his father and grandfather before him, he played in the court chapel at Rudolstadt (a small town in eastern Germany), and in 1792 he was appointed Kapellmeister. He devoted his time to composing, teaching, and—most relevant to us—writing books on music. His *Versuch einer Enleitung zur Composition* ('Introductory Essay on Composition') was written during the 1780s and it is the most approachable of the many composition manuals written at this time. He deals with real music by real composers, not artificial voice-leading exercises. He is up to date; he revised sections of the book to keep up with Mozart's innovations. And he is practical, when many other writers of the period seem interested primarily in questions of academic propriety.

In his *Essay,* Koch spends a lot of time talking about little dances like Example 31. Writing such dances was one of the standard exercises for budding composers, and composers like J. C. Bach and Mozart seem to have been churning them out almost as soon as they were out of nappies. The dance in Example 31 consists of a melody line and a bass, and it falls into two halves (that is, it is in **binary** form). It is made up of four

Ex. 31. Minuet from Koch's *Introductory Essay*

Harmony and Line

phrases each of four bars, with each pair of phrases making up an eight-bar section or *period*, as Koch calls it, and each period is repeated. (For Koch the essential attribute of a period is that it ends with a strongly marked cadence—'a formal cadence', to use his words.) We can summarize the form by means of a simple analytical diagram (**Example 32**).

Ex. 32

Bar	1	5		9	13
Phrase	A	B	:‖:	C	A
Key	C				
Begins	I	I		V	I
Ends	V	I		I	I

As you can see, the first phrase comes back at the end (only with its cadence altered so that it ends in the tonic). But there isn't anything sacred about this AB :‖: CA pattern; in other pieces you can find patterns like AB :‖: CB, or AB :‖: AC, or even AB :‖: CD. In the same way, you can find different harmonic patterns. The first phrase will always begin on I and the last will always end on I, because the piece needs to begin and end on the tonic. But the first three phrases can equally well end on I or V, while the last three phrases can begin on I or V, or IV, or practically anything else.

This is tuneful, singable music, and one of the things that makes it so is the rhythmic *motif* in bars 1, 5, 9, and 13; each phrase perceptibly begins in the same way, even though the notes are different. There is also a kind of rhyming effect at the cadences; the rhythm of bars 3–4 is echoed at 11–12, and the rhythm of bars 7–8 is echoed at bars 15–16. This, too, helps to tie the music together in a satisfying manner.

If a rhythmic motif is one way of turning a series of notes into a tune, another is contour. Each of the phrases of Example 31 goes up and down, like a wave or an arch. That's obvious in a general sort of way. But we can see exactly how the contour works if we draw a graph of the music, putting in only those notes where the melody changes direction, and connecting them with diagonal lines (**Example 33**). These patterns, made up of waves within waves, clearly contribute a good deal to the ebb and flow that characterize

Ex. 33   a well-shaped melody.

But there is another essential element in the design of a Classical melody, and this has to do with the counterpoint between melody and bass line—the way the two come together to define the harmonic framework of the music. I've tried to show this in **Example 34**, which picks out the most important notes of both parts, and (like Example 28) reduces each phrase of the original to a single bar, so making it easier to see the overall pattern. What is the basis on which I have selected these notes and no others? In general the most important notes come on the *downbeats*, so that is one criterion. A second criterion is that the notes which outline the cadence of each phrase are bound to be important. Most important, however, is the idea of bringing out the pattern of harmonic change, the *harmonic rhythm*, that is implied in the music; perhaps the best way to

Ex. 34

approach this is to imagine that you are accompanying the music at the keyboard, in the manner of Assignment 10. (The notes that demand chordal accompaniment are in general the ones that should appear in the analysis.) The result of all this is a reduction that represents the harmonic direction and continuity of the original music in the most concise manner possible; this implies that, if you add Roman letters to it, they should outline reasonably sensible-looking progressions. These Roman letters will represent the structural harmonies of the music.

On the basis of Example 34 we can draw several conclusions about the relationship between melody and bass:

- One simple but important point has to do with the relationship between the contour of the two lines. Very often the two lines work in **contrary** motion—meaning that when one goes up, the other goes down. The first and last phrases are entirely made up of contrary motion; it is almost as if the bass was a reflection of the melody. To be sure, this doesn't happen all the time (look at the second and third phrases), but it still represents an idiomatic feature of the Classical style.

- Another equally simple and important point concerns the intervals between the two lines. More often than not phrases begin or end in octaves; you might expect that. What you might not expect is the number of thirds, or tenths, or seventeenths (I shall lump all of these together and call them tenths) between the two parts; the '10's between the staves mark them, and this preponderance of tenths between the outer parts is a very general feature of Classical music. The reason is simple: with tenths between the outer parts you have both the root and the third of a chord; this clarifies the harmony and gives a full sound. (Parallel sixths between the outer parts are also very common, for the same reason.)

- Although the music is in only two parts, it generally makes the harmonies quite explicit. Because of this, it could easily be performed in the style of a baroque solo sonata, with a violin taking the tune, a cello taking the bass line, and a harpsichord filling out the harmony.

- You can see how very simple the harmonic basis of the music is: just three chords, I, IV, and V, generally with one harmony per bar. The IVs generally function as

Harmony and Line

approach chords to the cadence; the one phrase that doesn't have a IV, the third, lacks a definite cadence.

Example 34 is useful because it's the most important notes, and only the most important notes, that govern the counterpoint between melody and bass. And this means that if you want to add a bass line to an existing melody, it is a good idea to start by deciding what the most important notes of the melody are, and then designing your bass round them. I can give a practical demonstration of this by using **Example 35,** another dance tune which Koch gives in his *Essay*, but this time without a bass. Any resemblance between the top stave in **Example 36** and a well-known Christmas carol is purely coincidental; it is intended as a reduction of Example 35, made along the same lines as Example 34, and as such I hope it is more or less self-explanatory. (Bear in mind, incidentally, that you don't have to write the music out to make an analysis of this kind; you could just add extra long tails to the notes in the score, perhaps adding beams to group together the notes within each phrase.)

Ex. 35 Minuet from Koch's *Introductory Essay*

Ex. 36

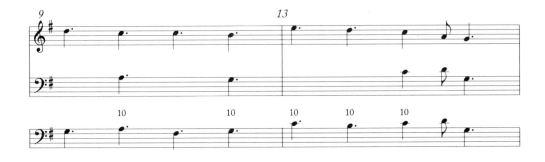

Cadences represent points of arrival, and harmonic progressions in Classical music are designed to lead towards these points of arrival. So it makes sense to settle on the cadence before dealing with the rest of the phrase. Stave (a) in Example 36 shows what this initial stage might look like. I'll comment on each cadence in turn:

- There isn't really any choice about the I at the end of the first phrase. V would be compatible with the D in the melody, but the previous melody note (E) doesn't make much sense as an approach to V. And given I, the only approach chord that can reasonably support the E is IV, creating a *plagal* cadence. It would, however, be possible to cadence on a root position I instead of I⁶ (that is, to have G instead of B on the final note), which would make the cadence rather more definite.

- Similarly, there is no choice about the V at the end of the second phrase. Given the E in the melody, the two possible approach chords are II and IV. An A in the bass is possible here, but the C creates a fuller sound (because the chord has a third) as well as leading smoothly to the D.

- As in Example 34, the third phrase does not have a definite cadence. The A and G are added tentatively on the basis of movement in tenths with the melody; the notes on the previous beats (as yet undecided) will need to lead to them.

- Finally, the V–I cadence at the end of the fourth phrase is more or less obligatory, and the IV approach echoes the cadence of the second phrase.

The next stage is to fill in the remainder of the bass line, as in stave (b). This is remarkably straightforward, because so much of the bass line can be worked in tenths with the melody. The only exception is the third phrase, where parallel tenths would be rather insipid in the absence of a definite cadence; the solution I have offered uses a contrary-motion approach to the A and the G. We now have a rough outline for the entire bass that fits well with the main notes of the melody.

We now need to find out how well this bass line fits with the details of the original melody. **Example 37** tests this. Stave (a) is essentially the same as stave (b) in Example 36, though it includes one or two small improvements (see bars 1, 4, 7, and 15). Everything fits adequately; this is a perfectly correct solution. But the conjunction of the two lines suggests a number of worthwhile refinements and elaborations, and these are incorporated in stave (b) of Example 37, as follows:

- Bars 2–3 of the bass line are based on the same G–A–B–C as bars 1–2 of the melody. This gives us the opportunity of introducing *imitation* between the two parts: the bass follows the melody line exactly, only a bar later. To bring out the imitation, we eliminate the bass line in the first bar; the melody can perfectly well stand by itself.

- Bar 4: the B–A–B–G in the bass serves to link the first phrase smoothly to the second. A similar motif continues through the next two bars, creating a pleasing rhythmic counterpoint between the two parts and bringing out the sequence in bars 6 and 7.

- Bar 7: the C♯ is a chromatic passing note, filling in between C♮ and D, and emphasizing the sense of arrival at the cadence.

- Bars 9–12: notice how the bass line has a distinctive rhythmic shaping in these bars. I couldn't resist changing the G in bar 9 to G♯, giving a pair of V⁷–I motions—first in A minor (bars 9–10), and then in G major. This kind of chromatic inflection is explained properly in the next chapter.

- The bass in bar 12 links the third phrase to the fourth; the dissonant relationship

Ex. 37

between the parts on the second beat sounds fine, because the counterpoint between the main notes of each line makes sense.

I'm not suggesting that you need go through this entire procedure every time you want to add a bass line to a melody. If a bass line comes to you straight away, and you think it sounds good, then write it down without more ado. But if it doesn't, the procedure I've described gives you a systematic way of approaching the problem.

How far do the rules of Classical part-writing apply to these two-part textures? As far as they apply to any Classical music, because the parts are totally exposed.

ASSIGNMENT 12 □

The worksheet shows two dance tunes by Mozart. In each case:

- *Make a tabular analysis, using Example 32 as a model; set it out the same way and include the same information.*
- *Add a bass line. Note that the opening four bars of the first tune form a sequence: bars 3–4 are the same as bars 1–2, only a step lower. Try to reflect this in your bass line.*

Ex. 38 Melody from Koch's *Introductory Essay*

In a way it's easier to write a melody and bass line together than it is to add a bass to an existing melody, because you aren't tied down. But in another way, the fact that you aren't tied down actually makes the task more difficult. Perhaps the most straightforward situation is when you have the beginning of a piece and want to complete it. **Example 38** comes from Koch's *Essay*, and is intended as the first half of a sixteen-bar minuet. To complete it, you would have to decide which (if any) of its phrases to use, and where. The first phrase is really too emphatic to be used for the third phrase, but it could be used for the fourth, with an alteration to the cadence so that the melody reaches C at the beginning of the final bar; this would give an AB :‖: CA plan. Alternatively, the second phrase could be used for the final phrase, with its cadence altered so that it ends on I; this would give an AB :‖: CB plan. So the job now becomes one of adapting whichever phrase you are going to reuse for the fourth phrase, and inventing the third phrase.

How do you invent a third phrase? You may find a useful rhythmic idea, or perhaps a melodic contour, in one of the previous phrases (see for instance Example 31). But the time will sooner or later come when you have to create something out of nothing, *ex nihilo*. How do you do this? Eighteenth-century theorists were familiar with this problem. In fact they had a special term for it: *inventio*, or the discovery of musical ideas. They distinguished this from *dispositio*, meaning the arrangement of existing ideas—the kind of adaptation and redistribution I was talking about in the previous paragraph. And they regarded *dispositio* as basically teachable, whereas *inventio* was basically unteachable: ideas, they said, either come or they don't. One or two theorists, however, came up with strategems for stimulating invention. In his *Elementi teorico-pratici di musica* ('Theoretical and Practical Elements of Music') of 1791–6, Francesco Galeazzi wrote:

We find many who can proceed with a given figure with little effort but who have insuperable difficulties when they have to invent new material. Here is something that can assist, with which one can discover a hundred, a thousand in the twinkling of an eye: it may appear puerile but first experiment with it and then judge.

And he tells you to write out the notes of the tonic triad on cards, and then choose one of them at random. Next you write out the seven notes of the scale on cards, and choose three or four of these, again at random. You experiment with different orderings of these notes, decide which is the best, and then use this as your basic material. Galeazzi gives some examples of his method in action (**Example 39**). The top stave shows three possible orderings of the same four notes; the staves underneath give examples of how each might be used.

Galeazzi uses his four notes exactly as they come; it is the characteristic rhythms that he imposes on them, and the way he continues them, that turn mere sequences of notes into tunes. But in his *Musikalisches Lexicon* (published in 1802), Koch shows another and perhaps more powerful method for drawing a wealth of characteristic material out a few notes—C, D, and E (**Example 40**). He treats his three notes as a melodic skeleton, elaborating them by interpolating other harmony notes between them (stave 1), weaving arpeggios round them (stave 2), and introducing passing and other non-harmony notes (staves 3–4). And of course you could combine these elaborations with any of the

Ex. 39 Galeazzi's system for melodic invention

Ex. 40 Koch's system
for melodic invention

Ex. 41

different counterpoints that are possible for C–D–E (**Example 41**). The possibilities are virtually endless.

But all this is only half the story—to be precise, the melodic half. As you work forward from the beginning of the phrase, inventing and testing and perhaps rejecting different melodic ideas, you also need to be thinking backwards from the cadence. And this means thinking harmonically. What chord are you going to cadence on? Are you going to approach it via IV, or perhaps II⁶? If II⁶, how are you going to approach it? Perhaps by a VI, giving a *cycle of fifths* progression (VI–II–V)? Perhaps by a I⁶, as in Example 36? By now, you will be thinking in terms of some such harmonic plan as I . . . VI–II⁶–V or I . . . I⁶–IV–V–I. What still remains is to fill in the gap represented by the dots.

There's a way of thinking about this that you may find helpful, and it is illustrated in **Example 42**. As you can see, it represents the whole process as a kind of pincers action, working simultaneously forwards from the beginning and backwards from the end. Let's suppose you want a phrase that begins on I and ends on V. You begin by writing these in on level (*a*). Then, on level (*b*), you start filling in the gap between the I and the V by expanding each of these chords. First you expand the V into a standard cadential progression: II⁶–V. Then you try expanding the initial I into one of those turn-the-handle sequence patterns that appear time and again in Classical music: I–V–VI–III–IV–I (a progression you will find in any keyboard harmony book, and most famously associated with Pachalbel's *Canon*). But you need to engineer a good join between this sequence pattern and the precadential II⁶; as Example 42 shows, one way to achieve this is by omitting the final I and moving directly from IV to II⁶. You now have a solid, coherent progression that should be able to support an equally coherent melody. All that is necessary is a bit of elaboration; (*c*) shows a possible result.

There's nothing magical about any of these methods for generating melodies and harmonies. Their main value is that they give you something to do, a way to get started.

Ex. 42

And they help to sort out the different tasks involved in writing music of this kind. The main difficulty with composition (and this perhaps applies to all composition, not just imitating the Classical style) is that you seem to have to decide everything at once. For instance, it's no good trying to write a melody without considering the bass. But equally, it's no good trying to write a bass without considering the melody. What this is likely to mean in practical terms is that you alternate between concentrating on the one and the other, and progress with a good deal of trial and error.

ASSIGNMENT 13 □

This assignment is in two parts.

- *Identify each occurrence of the following categories of melodic elaboration in Example 40 by writing the appropriate letter(s) above or below it: passing note (P), neighbour note (N), arpeggio or broken arpeggio (A), consonant skip (CS). A con-sonant skip means leaping from one note of a chord to another (if you have two consonant skips in a row, you call them an arpeggio, of course). Whereas P and N refer to notes, A and CS refer to intervals; use slurs to group the relevant notes together, as shown in the worksheet.*

- ***Example 43** is a reduction of another of the little dances Koch quotes in his book. Elaborate both the melody and the bass line to arrive at what you think might have been the original music, incorporating the opening given in the worksheet.*

Ex. 43

ASSIGNMENT 14 □

Complete the openings given in the worksheet as sixteen-bar dances for melody instrument and bass. (The first is the same as Example 38.)

ASSIGNMENT 15

Write any number of sixteen-bar dances on the model of Example 31.

CHAPTER 4

Modulation and Chromaticism

Example 44 is another little movement from Heinrich Koch's *Introductory Essay on Composition*; it is sixteen bars long and has the same form as the minuets we looked at in Chapter 3. However, this movement has one feature the others didn't: it modulates to V at the end of the second phrase.

I mentioned modulation in the Introduction, but it's worth underlining the difference between modulating to V and merely cadencing on it. As usual, we need an illustration. The second phrase of the minuet in Example 35 ended with an imperfect cadence, IV–V.

Ex. 44 Minuet from Koch's *Introductory Essay*

As the Roman letters indicate, the key didn't change: the phrase was harmonically open, demanding a continuation. Example 44 is quite different. Here the second phrase ends with a perfect cadence, V–I; again as the Roman letters indicate, it's a much more definite and conclusive cadence than the one in Example 35. But the V–I isn't in C major, the key in which the piece began; it is in G major. Somewhere in the first eight bars the music has moved from C major to G major; as a result, the G in bar 8 is not V of I, but I of V. We can express this by saying that the music has cadenced not *on* V, as was the case with Example 35, but *in* V. It is as if the idea of an imperfect cadence had been transferred from the note-to-note level to the larger level of key relations.

Just where did the music modulate? It all happens quite smoothly; there isn't a jolt between one key and the next. Everything up to the cadence at the end of bar 4 is clearly in C major. The second phrase starts out as if it were in C major, but by the F♯ of bar 6, the music clearly is in G major. The modulation happens, then, in bar 5 and the first half of bar 6. It's difficult to pinpoint because this passage in fact makes sense in both C major and G major. Seen in terms of C major, the old key, the C, G, and C chords (I'm assuming that the E on the second beat of bar 6 is the third of a C chord) are I, V, and I. Seen in terms of G major, the new key, the same chords are IV, I, and IV, and they lead to the V^7 on the final eighth note of the bar and the subsequent cadence. The music enters the progression as if it belonged to one key, and quits it as if it belonged to another; that's why the modulation happens so smoothly and unobtrusively. The analysis in Example 44 shows all this, and the box marks the passage during which the music makes sense in both keys. The chords within the box are known as ***pivot chords***, and the use of such chords represents the most important technique for modulation in Classical music.

Modulation plays a vital role in the large-scale Classical forms, as will become obvious in Chapters 10–12. Here I want to explore some of the ways that modulatory effects can be used on the small scale to create colour and tension, again using Example 44 for illustration. In his *Essay*, Koch gives a large number of alternative versions of bars 9–12 in order to show how many different harmonic patterns can be incorporated within a single phrase. He sets these out quite systematically, as shown in **Example 45** (where

Ex. 45

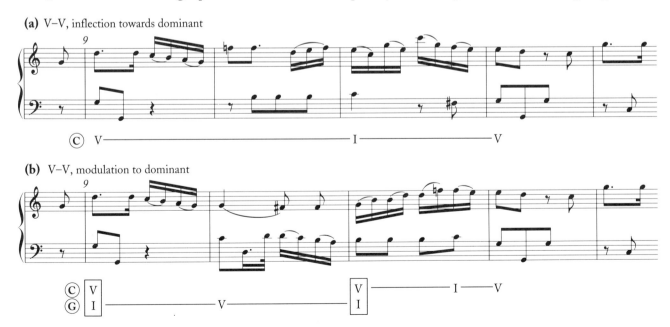

(a) V–V, inflection towards dominant

(b) V–V, modulation to dominant

however (*e*) and (*f*) are my own illustrations, replacing one of Koch's). I'll comment on each version in turn.

- In the original movement (Example 44), bars 9–12 begin and end on V, and there are no chromatic notes. In fact the only harmonies are I and V.

- Example 45*a* also begins and ends on V, and there are no real harmonies except I and V. But there is a tiny splash of G major colour in the F♯ at the end of bar 3. We can call this faint suggestion of another key an *inflection*.

- (*b*) modulates to G major, approached and quitted through pivot chords.

- (*c*) modulates to D minor, approaching it via its own V (the A major chord at the beginning of bar 2), and quitting it by means of a pivot chord. In fact the chord in bar 1 creates the effect of a pivot chord, though an ambiguous one; at the beginning of the bar it sounds like a I⁶ of C, whereas by the end of the bar it sounds more like a II (or possibly VII) of D minor. Ambiguous effects like this come about easily when the music is in only two parts.

- (*d*) also modulates to D minor, but incorporates a melodic and harmonic sequence. Both the melody and the bass in bars 3–4 are one step lower than in bars 1–2, and so the harmonic progression also repeats itself a scale step lower—first II–V–I of D minor, then II–V–I of C major. This progression appears time and time again in Classical music.

- (*e*) modulates through A minor. It is more complicated, in the sense that three keys are involved: C major, A minor, and G major. Although the moves from A minor to G major, and from G major back to C major, are accomplished through the use of pivot chords, there is no pivot between C major and A minor in bar 1. Here the modulation is achieved in a different way: the G at the beginning of the bar (the root of V of C major) is altered on the second beat to G♯ (the third of V of A minor). Instead of there being an overlap, the one key supplants the other. As you can see from **Example 46a**, what ties the progression together is the combination of the G–G♯ in the bass with the D in the melody, which changes from being the fifth of a G chord to the seventh of an E chord; this kind of ***chromatic alteration*** is the second most important technique for modulation in Classical music. Example 46*b* shows how the same pattern can work upside down, while (*c*) and (*d*) show a similar approach to II. Deft manipulation of leading notes and sevenths (what are sometimes called the 'sensitive notes') plays a major part in creating convincing modulations.

Ex. 46

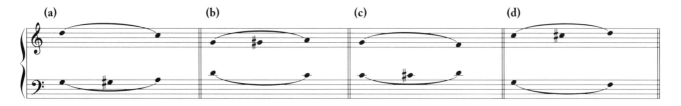

(a)   (b)   (c)   (d)

- (*f*) has exactly the same harmonic plan as (*e*), but introduces a sequence; as in (*d*), bars 3–4 are a step lower than bars 1–2.

- (*g*) passes through F major but is barely a modulation at all; only the B♭ in the melody of bar 2 needs to be analysed in F major. Notice the chromatic approach to the dominant in bar 3 (F♮–F♯–G).

- Finally, (*h*) begins in the same way as (*g*) but then continues with a sequence a scale step higher, giving the same V–I progression in F major and in G major. As in (*e*), there is no pivot chord between the two keys. But notice how easily Koch could have tied the whole phrase together by means of a chromatic motion in the bass (E–F♮–F♯–G); you could almost say that the chromatic motion is implied by the music, even though it doesn't actually appear.

There are two general observations I'd like to make about this series of examples. First, I've been talking of 'modulation' whenever there are a few chords that can't be analysed in terms of the main key. Many people prefer to restrict the term to larger-scale cases where a new key becomes firmly established as a tonic. When you are dealing with only a few bars you never really lose your sense of the main key, and for this reason it might be better to speak, for instance, of (*c*) **passing through** II of C major, rather than of its modulating to D minor. There's a useful notation that expresses this, according to which you would analyse this phrase as I–II(V–I)–V–I-V; the II(V–I) means a V–I progression *on II*. The term ***secondary dominant*** is used to refer to V chords that do not belong to the main key, such as V of II.

The second observation has to do with sequences. If you want to design a harmonic sequence like those in (*d*), (*f*), and (*h*), you need to begin with a coherent chord progression (CCP), such as V–I or II–V–I, that is two bars long. You use this progression on V for bars 3–4, and on anything else for bars 1–2, so the pattern works like this:

$$\textit{Bars} \quad\quad 1 \quad\quad\quad 3$$
$$X(CCP) \quad V(CCP)$$

where 'X' stands for any ***scale degree*** *except* V. The use of sequences for the third phrase of sixteen-bar pieces like Example 44 became so common in the eighteenth century that another composition teacher, Joseph Riepel, coined a special terminology for them. He called a rising sequence (like Example 45*h*) a *Monte* or rise, and a falling sequence (like (*d*) and (*f*)) a *Fonte*, or well. He also had a special term for a phrase that remained mainly on the dominant, like (*a*); this was a *Ponte*, or bridge.

ASSIGNMENT 16 □

This assignment is in two parts.

- *The worksheet shows six alternative versions of bars 9–12 from another dance quoted by Koch, this time in G major. Add a Roman-letter analysis to each of them, along the lines of Example 45. (The first has been worked as a guide.)*

- *Again using the worksheet, complete eight alternative versions of bars 9–12 of Example 31, modelling them on the eight passages in Example 45. This means that, in each case, you begin and end on the same harmony as Koch does, and pass through the same keys; it doesn't mean that you have to use exactly the same harmony at exactly the same point as Koch. Ensure that your versions fit well with what comes before and after. You can write in two parts, or three, or a mixture.*

ASSIGNMENT 17 □

This assignment is in two parts.

- *The worksheet shows one of the openings for a 16–bar dance from Assignment 14. Compose another completion of it, again for melody instrument and bass, but this time modulating to V in the second phrase, and passing through other keys in the third. It will help if you bear in mind that harmonic plans like I . . . VI–II⁶–V or I . . . I⁶–IV–V–I (discussed in Chapter 3) are easily adapted to end in a different key from the one they start in. You simply need to adapt them as follows:*

C: I . . . .

G: . . . .   I⁶–IV–V–I

- *Compose a 16-bar dance of your own, passing through a variety of keys.*

ASSIGNMENT 18 □

The worksheet shows the melody line of a minuet by Christian Scheinpflug, which Koch quotes in his Essay. (Scheinpflug was Koch's teacher, and his predecessor as Kapellmeister at Rudolstadt.) Koch does not give the bass line; add one.

ASSIGNMENT 19

Write a minuet and trio for small orchestra in the manner of Example 18.

When you see notes that do not belong to the main key of a piece, it means one (or both) of two things. The first is that there has been an inflection or modulation to another key. The second, which I'm going to discuss now, is that chromatic notes are being used within the main key, as a means of elaborating, modifying, or sometimes undermining the harmony. Chromatic passing notes, such as the F♮–F♯–G in Example 45*g*, represent a simple example of this. But chromaticism can be much more thoroughgoing, and nowhere more than in the music of Mozart. A representative example is the song *Der Frühling* ('Spring'), which dates from the same time as as *Das Kinderspiel* and paints an almost religious picture of the annual regeneration of nature. The text has several verses, all of which are set to the same music (that is, the song is **strophic**). **Example 47** shows the music, together with a Roman-letter analysis that picks out the structural harmonies.

This setting takes the form A–A–B–A, and its musical logic revolves round the three different statements of the opening phrase (bars 2, 6, and 14—the bar numbers are all one greater than you would expect, because bar 1 is an introduction). Each time the phrase appears, these bars are harmonized differently:

- On the last eighth note of bar 2, the C is harmonized with a V of V, suggesting that the music is going to continue along the lines of **Example 48**. As expected, there is a D in the bass on the first beat of bar 3, but it supports a diminished triad; and on the next eighth note the bass *falls* to D♭, supporting an E♭⁷ harmony. This functions as a secondary dominant to the chord at the beginning of bar 4, IV, with the bass falling further to C, so that the whole progression is contained within a diatonic I–IV relationship. In fact there are really no harmonies between the I and IV in a

Ex. 47 Mozart, *Der Frühling*, KV 597

Etwas langsam

1. Er - wacht zum neu - en Le - ben steht vor mir die Na - tur __ , und sanf - te Lüf - te we - ben durch

die ver - jüng - te Flur! Em - por aus sei - ner Hül - le drängt sich der jun - ge Halm; der

Wäl - der ö - de Stil - le be - lebt der __ Vö - gel Psalm.

Ex. 48

structural sense; there is just a series of chromatic passing notes in the bass (Eb–D–Db–C), supporting a series of **passing chords** in the upper parts.

- In bars 6–7, the V of V leads to a first inversion V, as expected, but this time the last two notes of the melody are Bb–Eb, not F–Bb. The dominant coloration is maintained, leading to a strong II–V–I cadence in the dominant at bars 8–9. As before, the progression in bars 6–7 is tied together with a stepwise descent in the bass (although this time it is diatonic, not chromatic).

- Bars 14–15 go back to the original melodic figure, but this time it is harmonized with three successive diminished seventh chords over a chromatically falling bass. As in the first phrase, this deeply expressive progression is contained within a diatonic relationship (this time I–II, initiating the II–V–I cadence), and the **conjunct** motion of the bass line helps to tie everything together.

Mozart's expressive harmonies, then, elaborate an underlying framework that is simple and diatonic; that is the essence of Classical chromaticism. In fact the basic chord functions in this song are just as limited as those of *Das Kinderspiel*—I, II, IV, and V (including I, II, IV, and V of V). This doesn't, of course, mean that the harmonies Mozart uses on a note-to-note level are limited in the same way—quite the opposite, in fact. The best illustration of this is bars 10–11 of *Der Frühling*. **Example 49** offers an analytical model of the successive levels of elaboration. At the most basic level (*d*) these bars consist simply of a dominant pedal, with the harmony moving from $^6_4$ to $^5_3$. The $^6_4$ is elaborated with a passing-note motion in the upper parts, falling from G/Bb to Eb/G (*c*). This in turn is elaborated by means of a regular sequence pattern: 3–6–3–6–3 (*b*). And finally this sequence pattern is itself elaborated by means of chromatic passing notes (*a*), creating the effect of a series of secondary dominants.

Ex. 49

To show how there is a simple diatonic framework underlying Mozart's richly chromatic harmony isn't to explain it away. The chromatic harmonies create colour, heighten the expression of the text (though Mozart doesn't use them for word-painting here), and contradict expectations. They are what is *characteristic* about this song. But they are at surface level. The music becomes bewildering if you try to understand it purely at this level, one chord at a time. Musical understanding comes from seeing how the chromatic harmonies arise from, and illuminate (or perhaps obscure), the underlying structure.

ASSIGNMENT 20

Examples 50 and **51** show two more songs by Mozart, written in 1785 and 1787 respectively. 'Die Zufriedenheit' means 'contentment' and the text says that even pain ('Schmerz') is agreeable when you are in love. 'Das Traumbild' describes a young man who lies in the countryside dreaming of a beautiful girl, and asks who she may be. Here is a summary analysis of 'Die Zufriedenheit', which divides it into phrases and picks out the most important harmonies. (The '=' signs represent pivot chords; see the fifth line down, where II in F is the same chord as VI in Bb).

'Die Zufriedenheit'

Bar	Key	Harmonies	Phrase structure	Text	
1	Bb	I–V	4+1	Piano intro	NB added bar
6		I–I	3+1	(continued)	
10		I–V	4+1	Lines 1–2	10–13 as 1–4
15		I–VI	4	Lines 3–4	
	F	=II–V–I			
19	Bb	V– I	4+1	Lines 5–6	20 cf. 11; 21–2 cf.
	F	=IV–V–I			12–13; 23 cf. 14
24	Bb	I–II⁶–V–I	4	Lines 7–8	24 cf. 10
28		I–II⁶–V–I	2+1	Piano postlude	cf. 7–10

- Based on 4-bar phrases but consistent play with irregularities.
- Consistent rhythmic pattern for final cadences of vocal phrases.
- Diatonic harmonies until 'Schmerz' (pain, bar 25); 'agreeable' resolution of chromatic harmonies at bars 26–7 mirrors text.
- Chromaticism gives a climactic quality to bars 24–7, heightened through register (the D and G of bars 24 and 25 are the lowest and highest vocal notes respectively; also note leap of 6th from Bb to G, bar 25).
- Melodic contours: each 4/5 bar phrase is arched, but large arched contours are 1–9, 10–18, 19–27; 28–30 is purely falling, heightening the conclusive effect.
- Piano texture: mainly homophonic. Varies from chordal accompaniment (e.g. 10) through simplified doubling (e.g. 13, 15) to full doubling (e.g. 11–12).

Make a similar analysis of 'Das Traumbild', using the same headings.

ASSIGNMENT 21

Write a song in Mozart's style using one of the following texts by Daniel Jägers for the first strophe.

> Einst lebte—so erzählet
> Der treue Mund der Zeit—
> Ein Mädchen, hiess Arete;
> O lebte sie noch heut',
> Ein Dutzend uns'rer Mägdlein
> Vertauscht' ich flugs dafür:
> So gut und schön sie scheinen,
> Hält kein's die Waage ihr.

(Once there lived—or so it's said—a maiden called Arete; if she were alive today, I'd trade twelve of our girls for her, so fair and good she was.)

> Wenn den langen Weg durchs leben
> Wir nun gingen so allein,
> Keine Seele um und leben;
> Freunde, wäre das wohl fein?
> Ich—das muss ich frei gesteh'n—
> Lieber wollt' ich gar nicht geh'n!

(If we have to go through life without company, my friend, is it all worthwhile? For myself, I must confess, I'd prefer not to go at all.)

Ex. 50 Mozart, *Die Zufriedenheit*, KV 473

Ex. 50 *cont.*

Ex. 51 Mozart, *Das Traumbild*, KV 530

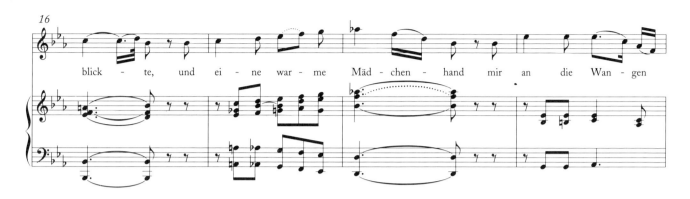

blick - te, und ei - ne war - me Mäd - chen - hand mir an die Wan - gen

drück - te?

CHAPTER 5

A Lesson from Mozart

IN the summer of 1785 a young Englishman, Thomas Attwood, arrived in Vienna to take composition lessons with Mozart. Attwood was a protegé of the Prince of Wales, who was paying for his education, and he stayed in Vienna until early 1787. When he returned to London, he took with him a large notebook consisting of the work that he had done with Mozart, complete with Mozart's corrections and occasional caustic comments ('you are an ass', Mozart scrawls when Attwood gets his clefs muddled up). The notebook is now in the British Library, and a transcription of it has been published as part of the *Neue Mozart-Ausgabe*.

Along with figured bass realization and studies in **strict counterpoint**, Mozart gave Attwood minuets for string quartet to complete. **Example 52** is a facsimile page of Attwood's notebook containing the first of these exercises, dating from 1785; it is at the top of the page, and **Example 53** is a transcription of it. In Example 53, as in later exam-

Ex. 52 Attwood Notebook, p. IV/3. Reproduced by permission of the British Library

Ex. 53

ples in this chapter, everything in large notes was written by Attwood; everything else was written by Mozart. (In the *Neue Mozart-Ausgabe* volume containing the Attwood workbook, everything written by Mozart is printed in red, and this makes it possible to pick out more detailed corrections by Mozart than can be shown here.) You can see that Mozart gave Attwood the first violin and cello parts for the first eight bars, and figured the bass to show the required harmonies; Attwood's assignment was to complete the inner parts for the first half of the minuet, and write the second half.

Attwood's first attempt wasn't very successful. In the first eight bars, there aren't actual mistakes, in the sense of impossible harmonies or blatant infringements of the conventions of part writing that I described in Chapter 1. The problem is just that both of Attwood's inner parts are deadly dull. It is one of the guiding principles of Classical chamber music that each player should have a part that not only makes sense in itself but is rewarding to play (in fact that is really the definition of chamber music); this isn't true of Attwood's parts. Another problem is the way the inner parts lurch upwards between bars 4 and 5, reflecting—rather than complementing—what happens in Mozart's outer parts. And the viola part sags on the last beat of bar 7, where moreover the chord lacks a third.

But the real problems lie in the second half that Attwood added. The first violin part immediately takes off into the stratosphere, returning to earth with the overstated double stops of bar 12; as you can see from Example 52, Attwood's lack of musical decorum at this point is reflected in his very handwriting. There are barely disguised parallel octaves between both the two inner and the two outer parts at bars 9–10 (Mozart has marked them with diagonal lines and crosses respectively). The parallel harmonies in bar 14 are awkward and the last two bars collapse unconvincingly into octaves. Under these circumstances, Attwood's attempt to show his sophistication by having the second violin imitate the first in bar 10 isn't really to the point. Mozart didn't bother to correct this attempt in detail. We can only imagine what he said to Attwood. The outcome, however, was that Attwood made a fresh attempt at the second half, and this is shown in **Example 54**.

Ex. 54

This time the first violin register is much more restrained, with the F–E♭ rising seventh in bar 13 (which was in Attwood's first attempt, where it derived from bars 9–10) now becoming the climax of the section. And the subdominant coloration nicely counter-balances the dominant harmony of bars 9–12. Mozart clearly felt that this was in essence a satisfactory solution. But he thought that some of the details could be improved. So he wrote out a revised version of Attwood's second attempt. He created more interesting inner parts by, in effect, swapping the second violin and viola in bars 10–11 (which allowed him to eliminate Attwood's doubled thirds), and again in bars 13–14. He made the viola's seventh in bar 12 resolve properly, that is downwards. He sorted out Attwood's registers in bars 13, where the second violin had got above the first (spoiling the rising seventh figure) and the viola below the cello. He improved Attwood's chord spacing in bar 15 and added a seventh to the cadence, so giving it a greater sense of finality. And lastly he added bowing marks, making the music *look* as if it was for string quartet.

ASSIGNMENT 22 □

The worksheet shows an assignment that Mozart set in 1784 for another of his pupils, Barbara Ployer, though she never completed it. (It was for Barbara Ployer that he wrote the piano concerto KV 453, in the same year.) Although it lacks double bars and repeat signs, it is a standard sixteen-bar minuet. Add second violin and viola parts. Bear in mind that you are not writing a Bach chorale; pedal notes and rests are idiomatic features of string quartet writing.

Despite his unpromising start, Attwood made good progress. Evidence of this is an exercise that Mozart set him the following year—a considerably harder exercise, with a lot of chromaticism (**Examples 55, 56**; the transcription is reconfigured so as to clarify the successive versions of bars 9–16). This time Mozart wrote the top line for the first half and the bottom line for the second half. Attwood had by this time studied a good deal of counterpoint and so he was quick to see how Mozart's lines were designed for imitation; the first thing he did was probably to write in the second violin part in bars 2–4 and the viola part in bars 10–12. After that the main problem will have been to work out just what harmonies Mozart's extremely chromatic lines imply. Unlike in the

Ex. 55 Attwood Notebook, p. IV/31. Reproduced by permission of the British Library

Ex. 56

previous exercise, Mozart didn't provide a figured bass: Attwood had to work the chords out for himself.

We can't know how he set about it, but we can guess. He probably worked phrase by phrase. Mozart's bowing marks highlight the sequential structure in the first four bars, so Attwood will have thought about the two-bar sub-phrases. Most probably he saw the harmonic pattern straight away, but if he didn't, he could have worked it out. The key to this is realizing that there is just one harmony per bar, and that there are accented passing notes on the downbeats. In fact, though it works across the beat, the melodic pattern is very clear: C–A, D–B♮; B♭–G, C–A. Once you've seen that, it's not too difficult to see the chords they imply: F, G; C⁷, F—that is, I, V of V; V⁷, I. That gives the lowest notes in these four bars, and instead of giving them all to the cello, Attwood shares them between the cello and viola. He even manages to introduce a bit of variation, with the viola's C–F (bars 3–4) answering the cello's G–G a bar earlier.

The second phrase is a bit more complicated. But its last two bars suggest II–V (Mozart in fact suggested a simple II in place of Attwood's slightly fussy setting of bar 7, as you can see from the correction on the right of the bottom system.) And the G–E–F in the bass at bar 6 is one of those clichés that you see time and again as a counterpoint for a chromatic descent. That only leaves bar 5; here there's no compellingly obvious harmonic progression, and so Attwood has written a linear cello part moving in contrary motion to the melody. Finally the inner parts are filled in, using large numbers of diminished seventh chords; the slightly oily quality of some of Mozart's chromatic textures remained as a permanent feature of Attwood's compositional style.

Whether or not he went about it this way, Attwood completed the first half of the minuet so well that Mozart found very little to correct. But in the second half Attwood made a number of errors. One was to put the imitation in the viola, resulting in a dull line at the top of the texture; Mozart rewrote bars 9–12 at the bottom of the page, transferring the imitation to the first violin. The other errors have to do with what Attwood *did* give the first violin in these bars. He wrote a C♯ in bar 9 and a B♮ in bar 11, in each case giving an augmented sixth with the cello; Attwood seems to have had a weakness for **augmented sixth chords**, for he introduced them at any available opportunity. (An augmented sixth chord is a VI with the addition of a sharpened sixth, used as an approach chord to V; see **Example 57**.) Mozart used augmented sixth chords, of course. But he would surely have avoided introducing the C♯, a dissonant note, in a prominent register and without any kind of preparation; the note comes out of the blue. (It would

Ex. 57

Attwood

II (VI♯⁶ — V ——— I)   ♭VI♯⁶ — V ——— I

Mozart

II (V⁷ ——————— I)   V⁷ ——————— I

have been all right if it could have been approached by step.) He would also have avoided the awkward *cross relation* with the cello's C♮ on the previous beat, and the yawning gap between the two parts.

By comparison with Mozart's solution (given at the bottom of the page), Attwood's seems over-complicated. As Example 57 shows, Attwood has two chords in each of bars 9 and 11; he harmonizes the E♭ independently of the D, and the D♭ independently of the C. By contrast, Mozart has one chord in each bar, with double suspensions. And in this way Mozart clarifies the basic progression of bars 9–12, in a way that Attwood does not: V–I of II, followed by V–I. It is the same, familiar progression as in Example 45*d*.

What happened to Attwood after he finished studying with Mozart? He returned to England and enjoyed a successful career. Among other posts, he was organist at St Paul's Cathedral, London, and composer at the Chapel Royal. He wrote mainly anthems, songs, and music for the stage. And when the Royal Academy of Music was founded in 1823, Attwood was among its first professors. He died in 1838, leaving behind him an unfinished anthem for the coronation of Queen Victoria.

ASSIGNMENT 23

*Attwood completed a number of further exercises after Example 56, and **Examples 58** and **59** are transcriptions of two of them. In both cases, all four parts are by Attwood; but Mozart has corrected them, rewriting the whole of Example 58 and parts of Example 59. Write a short essay on each of these exercises, explaining the problems in Attwood's version and the point of Mozart's revisions.*

ASSIGNMENT 24 ☐

The worksheet shows another assignment that Mozart set Barbara Ployer. Complete the inner parts. This is an exercise in chromatic harmony and suspensions; base what you write on Mozart's figures.

ASSIGNMENT 25 ☐

A third assignment for Barbara Ployer is shown in the worksheet. Here Mozart has written only the first half of a minuet, but he has provided three alternative bass lines of increasing complexity. (The third is an exercise in diminished sevenths that would have delighted Attwood.) Add inner parts to each version, basing what you write on Mozart's figures, and complete the minuet.

ASSIGNMENT 26

This assignment is in two parts.

- One of the features of string quartet writing is the variety of textures that can be obtained from grouping the instruments in different ways. A good illustration is **Example 60**, which is taken from a quartet that Mozart wrote in 1773 (the excerpt ends with the return of the opening section). Different groupings begin at bars: beats 1:1, 2:3, 4:3, 6:3, 8:3, 9:1, 13:1, 17:1, 20:3, 24:3, 27:2, 32:3, 34:3, 38:3, 40:3. Indicate the grouping at each of these points, using the following code. (You can work this assignment by simply writing out the bar numbers, together with the appropriate code letter.)

(a)	(b)	(c)	(d)	(e)	(f)	(g)	(h)	(i)
vn. 1				vn. 1	vn. 1	vn. 1	vn. 1	vn. 1
		vn. 2	vn. 2	vn. 2	vn. 2	vn. 2	vn. 2	vn. 2
	va.	va.	va.	va.	va.	va.	va.	va.
			vc.	vc.	vc.	vc.	vc.	vc.

- **Example 61** is a transcription of another minuet for string quartet that Mozart wrote in the same year, but never integrated into a finished work. Try to reconstruct the original string quartet score.

Ex. 58

Ex. 58 *cont.*

Ex. 59

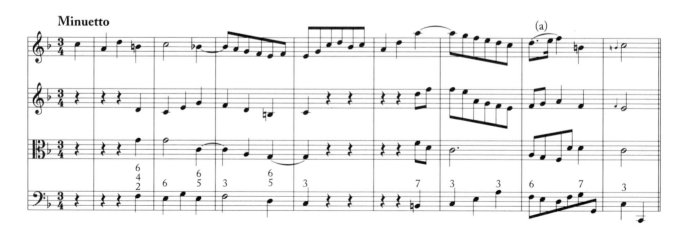

Ex. 59 *cont.*

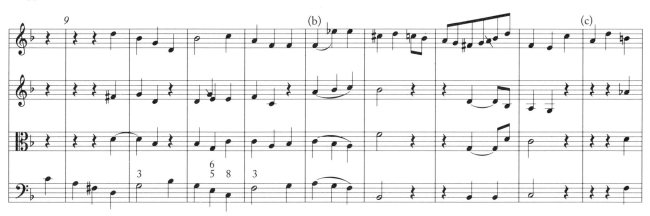

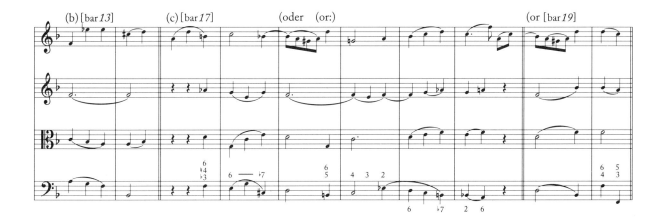

Ex. 60 Mozart, quartet movement, KV 158

Ex. 60 *cont.*

Ex. 61 Mozart, quartet movement (transcription)

Part III

Variation and Expansion

Introduction to Part III

VARIATION is like arrangement and accompaniment: it is based on analysis. Variation sets begin with something called the 'theme', but that is rarely, if ever, what they actually vary. Rather, they vary the basic melodic or harmonic structure that underlies the so-called theme. Like arrangement and accompaniment, then, writing variations develops theoretical concepts in a practical context.

But that is not the only reason for studying it. Variation is one of the absolutely central compositional techniques not just of Classical music, but of the music of almost all times and places. There are few other compositonal techniques of Classical music of which the same can be said. (What is generally called common-practice harmony, for instance, is far more restricted in both historical and geographical scope.) The very different types of variation found in different musical styles all have one thing in common: they combine the familiar with the new. They offer repetition without boredom, invention without incoherence. Because of this, variation is one of the most listener-friendly of all compositional techniques.

Variation sets, consisting of a theme plus an indefinite number of varied repetitions of it, demonstrate the Classical variation technique in the clearest possible manner, and so these form the focus of Chapters 6 and 7. But variation is by no means restricted to variation sets. It is at work throughout the whole of the Classical repertory, from the varied repeats of miniature dance forms to the development sections of solo sonatas and symphonies. It is one of the essential means for creating continuity in the Classical style. In itself, however, the variation principle does not create length; it operates within a given frame. So Chapters 8 and 9 introduce the two complementary principles that are used in Classical music to create length. One is the principle of modular expansion; the other is the principle of flexible prolongation.

The modular principle involves chopping a piece of music into bits (the proper term for this is 'segmentation') and reconfiguring the bits in new ways. If they are repeated (and perhaps varied), or if new material is interpolated between them, then the piece of music will obviously become longer. Heinrich Koch's *Introductory Essay on Composition* includes a detailed description of this technique, showing how miniature dances can be expanded stage by stage into full-length sonata style movements. What gives added interest to Koch's account is that there are a number of works by Haydn, written around the time of Koch's manual, that embody very much the kind of technique Koch talks about:

at times you almost get the impression that Haydn has been reading Koch. The musicologist Elaine Sisman has made a special study of the relationship between Koch and Haydn, and my account is based in part on her work.

The modular technique is rather like creating a mosaic: small, inflexible fragments are combined to make the big picture. What I have called the principle of flexible prolongation is just the opposite: it could be compared to stretching a rubber band. The clearest illustration of this principle is the cadenza, which in essence consists of a pause on the dominant that is stretched out, spun out, through a series of melodic elaborations. Musical time, with its symmetries of phrase and rhythm, stands still; a cadenza is the prolongation of a single moment. And just as the variation principle is not restricted to variation sets, so the prolongation principle is not restricted to cadenzas. It too is found throughout Classical music, especially in development sections and those passages traditionally called 'transitional'. (These terms will be explained properly in the final section.) In fact the two principles that I have described for creating length—the modular principle and the prolongation principle—can be seen as operating in a kind of counterpoint with one another throughout all the longer compositions of the Classical repertory.

The term 'prolongation' is closely associated with the analytical approach introduced in the first half of the twentieth century by the Austrian pianist and theorist, Heinrich Schenker. And Schenker's graphing technique, which sees music as made up of successive levels of elaboration, lends itself particularly well to the analysis of cadenzas. (Example 90 is in essence a Schenkerian analysis, though it lacks some of the refinements of the real thing.) Once seen as the preserve of specialists and enthusiasts, Schenkerian analysis has become the most widely accepted technique for the advanced analysis of Western tonal music. An adequate introduction to Schenkerian graphing technique, and the theory that underlies it, is beyond the scope of this book. (Some introductory texts are mentioned in the Conclusion.) It is, in any case, unnecessary for present purposes. Like German, Schenkerian analyses are easier to read than to write; once you have grasped the basic idea, it is not too hard to see what they mean.

Further Reading

- The source for Kirnberger's and other musical dice games (Chapter 6) is again Leonard Ratner's *Classic Music:*

Expression, Form, and Style, together with his article 'Ars Combinatoria' (in H. C. Robbins Landon and Roger Chapman (eds.), *Studies in Eighteenth-Century Music* (London, 1970), 343–63). As Ratner makes clear, while these dice games may be of marginal importance in themselves, they are symptomatic of an approach to music as pattern that was central to Classical composition.

- For Elaine Sisman's work on Koch and Haydn, see her 'Small and Expanded Forms: Koch's Model and Haydn's Music', *Musical Quarterly*, 68 (1982), 444–75. Sisman discusses the movement from Haydn's Symphony No. 14 at some length.

- The quotation from Czerny in Chapter 9 is taken from Alice Mitchell's translation of his *Systematic Introduction to Improvisation on the Pianoforte* (New York, 1983), 2. This provides a fascinating glimpse of the startlingly unfamiliar world of piano performance a hundred and fifty years ago.

CHAPTER 6

Varying a Line

SIXTEEN-BAR dance forms may be very good for teaching people how to compose, but they are not much use for anything else: what can you *do* with a piece that is only sixteen bars long? The answer, of course, is that you can make it longer. One way to do this is to repeat some of the phrases and interpolate new ones, so that you end up with a longer continuous movement—that's what Chapter 8 is about. But this and the next chapter are about the other way to turn short into longer pieces, which is to repeat them with alterations, and then to repeat them again with more alterations, and so on—in other words, to make variation sets out of them.

As you might expect from Chapter 5, Mozart set Attwood some exercises in variation. These make a good starting point for looking at variation technique, because they involve variation of an unusually systematic nature. **Example 62** shows one of them. It consists of adding a number of different bass lines to the same eight-bar melody, with each successive bass line moving twice as fast as the previous one. (I have set out the music in such a way that you can easily see the relationship between the different versions.) You can work out the order in which things happened. Mozart began by writing the tune; for his first exercise, Attwood had to add a bass line in quarter notes, complete with figures. Mozart corrected this, altering some of the figuring. (He deleted Attwood's '3's because they are redundant; the other changes are self-explanatory.) All this is in (*a*). Next, Mozart wrote out the first bar of two further exercises, using the same tune, but with the bass moving in eighth notes in (*b*), and in sixteenth notes in (*d*). Attwood worked both these exercises, rewriting his working of the eighth-note exercise at (*c*), and finally Mozart corrected both (*c*) and (*d*).

I've described this as an exercise in variation, and certainly it involves systematically varying the bass line. But Attwood would have thought of what he was doing in the light of strict or species counterpoint. This was a way of teaching composition that was widely used throughout the eighteenth century. It was first set out in 1725 by Johann Fux in an extremely influential treatise called *Gradus ad Parnassum* (there is an advertisement for the English translation at the bottom of Example 2), and it involved writing exercises in a kind of watered-down Renaissance style, more or less along the lines of Palestrina. You began, as Renaissance composers often did, with a ***cantus firmus***—a given melodic line, perhaps taken from an ecclesiastical plainchant, or perhaps invented. Then you had to add one or more lines to this. There was a systematic progression from one species to the next. In the first species the different lines went at the same speed, and you were only allowed to use ***consonances*** between them—that is, thirds, fifths, sixths, and unisons or octaves. In the second species, you added a part that moved twice as fast as the cantus firmus, keeping to consonant intervals on the main beats but interpolating passing notes or neighbour notes between them. The third species was the same, except that your added part moved four times as fast as the cantus firmus. In the fourth species you introduced suspensions, and in the fifth and final species you could use any of these techniques.

Ex. 62

Species counterpoint wasn't intended as a method for creating real music (in the way that Schoenberg's serial method was). It was a way of teaching, not a way of composing. Its message was that simple, consonant formations were the basis of all music. Dissonant harmonies and complex textures were to be understood as elaborations of simple, consonant formations. This didn't mean that, when you composed, you had to work out the elaborations one by one. You mightn't even be consciously aware of the simple, consonant basis of what you were writing. But it would still be guiding your actions, ensuring the coherence of what you wrote. If you weren't consciously aware of it, that was because it had become an ingrained habit of mind. Species counterpoint, in short, taught a way of *thinking* about music. And because this way of thinking about music was so fundamental to the Classical style, species counterpoint persisted as a teaching method right through the Classical period. Haydn actually used *Gradus ad Parnassum* in his teaching. Mozart set Attwood exercises in species counterpoint. Beethoven had a thorough grounding in it from his teacher, Johann Albrechtsberger.

Example 62 is not an exercise in strict counterpoint, but you can see how it is based on the same idea. Each note in the bass line of (*a*) is a harmony note; this corresponds to the principle, in first species counterpoint, of using only consonances. By contrast, (*b*) resembles second species counterpoint. In the first bar of (*b*), written by Mozart, the bass line contains all the notes of Attwood's bass line from (*a*), with other notes interpolated between them; the C, E, and G appear on the beat, but the final C has been shifted to the last eighth note of the bar. When Attwood takes over, in bar 2 of (*b*), he tries to follow Mozart's pattern exactly: the B, C, and F from (*a*) appear on the first three beats, and the E on the last eighth note. But Attwood is not happy with the second half of the bar, perhaps because the F (the seventh of an implied V^7) does not resolve properly. So he changes the F and G to D and B. But the line is still not very satisfactory: it seems to go round in circles, because of the repetition of C–E on the second and fourth beats, and the B–C in the bass creates parallel octaves with the main notes of the melody. Attwood might have done better to leave the F and G as they were, and instead change the last two notes to E–D.

In bar 3, Attwood starts off by being more adventurous. Instead of his original bass line, C–B–A–G, he writes an ascending line: the C, B, A, and G all appear, but the last three notes are an octave higher. However, Attwood is not happy about the way his bass outlines a seventh (C-E-G-B). So when he reworks his answer in (*c*), he replaces the whole of this bar. But the new version is a something of a cop-out. It simply consists of the original quarter notes, alternating with the higher octave. Mozart rejects this solution, and offers two better ones on the staves below; one consists of alternating thirds, while the other is based on parallel sixths and introduces a little inflection towards E minor. It looks as if Mozart preferred the last of these solutions, because this is the one he used as a model in his corrections to (*d*), adding passing notes between the thirds.

ASSIGNMENT 27

Complete the analysis of Example 62, reconstructing the way in which Attwood worked the exercise and explaining Mozart's corrections.

ASSIGNMENT 28 □

Mozart set a similar exercise for Barbara Ployer; it is shown in the worksheet. I have added part of a bass line in quarter notes. Complete this, then write a bass line in eighth notes, and finally one in sixteenths. Observe the sequences in bars 1–2 and 5–6, and bring out the move to V in bar 4. You need not add figures.

Example 63 shows the theme and first five variations of the finale of a divertimento which Haydn wrote in the early 1760s; it is called 'Der Geburtstag', probably because it was written to celebrate the birthday of one or another member of the Esterházy family. It is for a little orchestra consisting of flute, oboe, two violins, cello, and bass; although there aren't figures on the bass, the texture seems to demand a harpsichord continuo as well. These little orchestras tended to be thrown together on an *ad hoc* basis, and Haydn may well have found himself in the position of a school music director today, who finds himself faced with players of widely varying ability; at least that's what the variations suggest, for the oboe variation is almost exaggeratedly easy, whereas the flute variation requires nifty tonguing and the variation for first violin is positively virtuosic.

All these variations (as well as three variations not shown in Example 63, which are for the whole ensemble) are built on the same, unchanging bass line. So this is the mirror image of the exercise Mozart gave Attwood, where the melody remained the same

Ex. 63 Haydn,
Divertimento a Sei,
Hob. II: 11 ('Der
Geburtstag')

while the bass changed. Now varying a melody and varying a bass line involve rather different techniques. The main difference is that, while you can make bass lines move faster, you cannot change or omit the notes that define the basic harmony; that is why the essential technique for varying bass lines is interpolation. But you can be much more flexible in your treatment of melodies, especially when there is a continuo instrument

Finale: Thema con variazioni
Thema - Moderato

Var. 1

Ex. 63 *cont.*

Var. 4

Var. 5

filling in the harmonies. There is usually a range of possible counterpoints to any given bass, and you can choose one or another, or swap between them, adding or omitting notes at will.

This has an effect on how you set about writing variations. If you are varying a bass line, you simply take what you are given, and elaborate it. But this doesn't usually work very well with melodies. Melodic variations aren't generally so much variations *on* a given melody, but variations *of* it. What I mean by this is that you don't elaborate the melody as such; you elaborate the structural framework that lies behind it. In other words, you begin by analysing the melody, stripping of its surface detail, and then you reconstruct it by adding new elaborations. Example 63 illustrates this very well. If you look at the first few bars in each variation, you will see that they aren't very like the theme at all. In fact, at first glance, you might well question in what sense they *are* variations on the theme, other than that they all go with the same bass line.

Example 64 provides the answer to this question, by reducing the first four bars of each variation to its underlying structure. As you can see, the different variations have a number of features in common at this underlying level. In the first bar, three of them share the same basic melodic pattern: G–F–E. But that doesn't really help, because this pattern isn't found in the theme! In bar 2, all the variations share the F and E with the theme, but the other notes are variable. And in bar 3 it is difficult to see any pattern at all; only Variations 1 and 5 are similar. What is going on? The answer is that we have a variety of possible counterpoints with the unchanging bass line. For instance, the first four notes of the theme move in parallel sixths with the bass, whereas the first four notes of Variations 3 to 5 move in parallel tenths with it. And on the first and fourth beats of bar 2, where the bass has the third of the chord, some of the variations add the root while others add the fifth. The result is a plurality of possible melodic patterns.

In a real sense, then, the different variations don't vary the theme at all; it would make as much sense to call the theme 'Variation No. 0' instead. The only difference in the

Ex. 64

so-called theme, apart from the fact that it comes first, is that it presents its particular counterpoint with the bass in a very simple manner; there is a little rhythmic displacement as against the regular eighth notes in Example 64, but that is all. The other variations offer more in the way of elaboration, with each variation introducing its own characteristic pattern. In addition to rhythmic displacement (notes being shifted forward or back in time), there is registral displacement (notes being shifted up or down an octave, most obviously in Variation 2). A special type of rhythmic displacement is **syncopation**, as in Variation 3; and a special type of syncopation is illustrated by Variation 1, where there are *chains of suspensions*. Apart from these, there are just the usual melodic elaborations—passing notes, neighbour notes, appoggiaturas, and consonant skips. And of course there are repeated notes, which are a special feature of Variation 2. Everything Haydn does can be brought under one or more of these headings.

On the basis of all this, it's possible to formulate a protocol for writing melodic variations:

- The first step is analytical: you strip off any melodic elaboration in the theme, revealing the basic two-part counterpoint.

- After familiarizing yourself with the phrase and harmonic structure of the theme, you write as many other counterpoints with the bass as you can think of, in the manner of Example 64. This produces a repertory of underlying melodic patterns.

- Next you create a repertory of surface patterns. Each will have its own characteristic rhythm, contour, articulation, or a combination of these features. In a variation set for orchestral instruments, like 'Der Geburtstag', one of the most important factors is clearly going to be what instrument the variation is for. (The oboe could not possibly play the flute variation in Example 62; the flute could play the oboe's, but it would not sound very effective.) So you will probably conceive each of your surface patterns in relation to a particular instrument.

- Finally, you match up your surface patterns with your underlying patterns, writing each variation fairly quickly and perhaps going back to polish it up at the end.

In practice, of course, you are likely to do these things simultaneously rather than in strict succession. Composing music is always messier in practice than in theory.

ASSIGNMENT 29

Example 65 *shows a theme that Mozart wrote in 1782, though he never completed any variations on it. (It was originally in C major.) Write the first half of two variations on Mozart's theme, for different melody instruments, and complete one of them. Like Haydn in 'Der Geburtstag', you should keep Mozart's bass line as it is. Assume there will be a harpsichord to fill out the harmonies.*

The variation principle provides the key to the musical games that were popular in the eighteenth century. The first of these was published in 1757 by the music theorist Johann Kirnberger, under the title *Der allezeit fertige Polonoisen- und Menuettencomponist* ('The Ever-ready Polonaise and Minuet Composer'). Others, in some cases very similar, were invented by C. P. E. Bach, Haydn, and Mozart (or at least they were published under these composers' names, which isn't always the same thing). The purpose of all these games is to allow you to compose a virtually unlimited number of pieces without need-

Ex. 65 Mozart, KV 383ᵈ, transposed

ing any musical skill, and they all work in essentially the same way. They present you with impressive tables of numbers, which refer to an equally impressive table of musical fragments; **Example 66** shows one of the tables of numbers from Kirnberger's game, the first seven of his musical fragments, and a sample realization. You compose your piece one bar at a time, by throwing a dice, beginning with the first section ('erster Theil'). If your first score is 2, you look along the top line of numbers ('1 Wurf', or first throw) until you come to the '2' column; there you read '63'. That refers you to number 63 in the table of musical fragments, which is the first bar of the sample realization. If you next throw a 5, you look along the next line of numbers until you come to the '5' column, and read '7', which gives you the second bar. And so on, until the first section is finished. Then you repeat the process with the second, giving a total of sixteen bars.

How do these games work? To create one, you need to write a theme and five variations on it (because a dice gives six possible scores). Each variation needs to be similar enough in style to the others (and to the theme) that you can take one bar from the first, the next bar from the second, the third bar from the theme, and so on, in any order, and still get a musically plausible result. You could now just write out your variations in a series, numbering the bars, so that the theme would begin at bar 1, the first variation at bar 17, the second at bar 33, and so forth. Then all you would need would be a table of numbers beginning like this:

Score	1	2	3	4	5	6
1st throw	1	17	33	49	65	81
2nd throw	2	18	34	50	66	82
3rd throw	3	19	35	51	67	83

Ex. 66 Kirnberger's
dice game. (*a*) and (*b*)
are from his *Der
allezeit fertige
Polonoisen- und
Menuettencomponist*;
(*c*) is a sample
realization

(a)

Tabelle zur Menuet mit einem Würfel.

	Erster Theil.						Zweyter Theil.					
	1	2	3	4	5	6	1	2	3	4	5	6
1 Wurf	23	63	79	13	43	32	33	55	4	95	38	44
2 = =	77	54	75	57	7	47	60	46	12	78	93	76
3 = =	62	2	42	64	86	84	21	88	94	80	15	34
4 = =	70	53	5	74	31	20	14	39	9	30	92	19
5 = =	29	41	50	11	18	22	45	65	25	1	28	17
6 = =	83	37	69	3	89	49	68	6	35	51	61	10
7 = =	59	71	52	67	87	56	26	91	66	82	72	27
8 = =	36	90	8	73	58	48	40	81	24	16	85	96

(b)

(c)

The trouble is that if the game were set out like this, everybody could see how it worked! So you chop up your variations into individual bars and set these out in a random order, altering your table of numbers so that each throw of the dice still refers to the same bar of music. (Kirnberger's division of the sixteen bars into two parts—really just bars 1–8 and 9–16—adds a further layer of obfuscation.) The result is that it seems like magic when each throw of the dice produces a bar that makes perfect harmonic and melodic sense with the previous one.

Is there a serious message in these games? Yes: they show the extent to which Classical music relied on standardized musical ideas that could be slotted together in different combinations. Modularity and symmetry are a precondition for games of this sort; it would be quite impossible to design an 'Ever-ready Prelude and Fugue Composer' along the same lines.

CHAPTER 7

Keyboard Variations

YOU can play music on a keyboard instrument without its necessarily being keyboard music. By keyboard music I mean music whose style and elaboration is specifically adapted to the keyboard, arising from the engagement of the fingers with the keys. The variations we shall be looking at in this chapter are all keyboard music in this sense.

The second movement of J. C. Bach's Sonata Op. 17 No. 1, which was published around 1774, is a set of variations for piano. It is shown (with a few gaps) in **Example 67**. Just from the look of the music on the page you can see that the variations make up a kaleidoscope of different figurations. The Minuet that serves as a theme is dissolved into different patterns of arpeggios and scales, with the note values getting smaller as the variations progress. In fact Bach's score looks rather like a set of studies for intermediate grade piano students. As in studies, each variation establishes a characteristic pattern—triplets in the right hand and chords in the left, or tune in the right hand and sixteenth notes in the left—which is maintained in more or less the same form throughout the variation. The figuration acts like a kind of filter through which the theme is passed.

To liken Bach's variations to studies may suggest that they are mechanical. In essence, that is exactly what they are. But Bach is careful to polish the details of the piano writing, and he also introduces a few irregularities into it; compare, for instance, bars 14 and 16 of Variation 1. Perhaps the most interesting example of such variety, however, is at the level of the overall organization of the variation set. If you look at the figuration patterns of the different variations you will see that there is *nearly* a very neat structure. As **Example 68** shows, everything is symmetrical (remember the *Min.* *D.C.* at the end), *except* for Variation 4. This variation is like nothing else; it is syncopated throughout, and full of dissonances. (Most remarkable is the simultaneous sounding of C♯ and C♮ at bar 9.) It doesn't stop the symmetrical plan of the variations being perceptible, but it prevents it being too obvious and therefore banal.

Ex. 67 J. C. Bach, Sonata Op. 17 No. 1, second movement

Minuetto con variazioni

Ex. 67 *cont.*

Var. 1

Var. 2

Ex. 67 *cont.*

Var. 3

Var. 4

Ex. 67 *cont.*

Var. 5

Min⁰. D.C.

Ex. 68

- Theme

Variation 1	LH: as theme	RH: triplets
Variation 2	LH: triplets	RH: as theme
Variation 3	LH: similar to theme	RH: sixteenth notes
Variation 4	(Interpolation)	
Variation 5	LH: sixteenth notes	RH: similar to theme

- Theme

As usual, the music is essentially in two parts; additional notes appear only sporadically, as for instance in the first chord, where they simply create dynamic emphasis. (This is a stylistic feature going back to the harpsichord, on which the only way to make more noise is to hit more keys.) Neither the melody nor the bass line of the theme are retained in any literal form throughout the whole set, though at any one time *either* the melody *or* the bass appears in more or less its original form. The bass line is varied in very much the manner of Attwood's exercises: you can almost always find the original notes somewhere in the left hand figuration of Variations 2 and 5, and usually on the beats rather than off them. Similarly, the main contours of the melody (such as the descent from D to G in the first and last phrases) are usually to be found somewhere within the right hand figuration; Bach often puts the melody in the thumb and first finger, with the rest of the figuration coming *above* it.

Composers of Bach's generation still thought in terms of figured bass, and one of the best ways to approach a piece like this is to play through it rather as if you were realizing a continuo part. Begin by playing the theme as if it were one of those Mozart songs with just a melody and a bass line, putting the chords in the right hand with a simplified version of the tune on top. Then play through the variations, reducing the arpeggios and scales to block chords, but keeping the same hand positions as in the original (whether in the right or the left hand); for instance, you would play the beginning of Variation 1 as shown in **Example 69b**. This is a good way to develop a feel for the music. It is also a simple way of generating variations. Try altering the hand positions, moving the hand up or down a notch, as in (*c*). And having done that, elaborate your new block-chord version with something more or less like Bach's figuration pattern, or invent new figuration patterns of your own, as in (*d*) and (*e*). The idea is to find yourself almost improvising Bach's variations, recapturing the way in which (as I said) they arise from the engagement of the fingers with the keys.

Ex. 69

(a)

(b)

(c)

Ex. 69 *cont.*

(d)

(e)

ASSIGNMENT 30

This assignment is to be worked at the keyboard, and is in two parts.

- *Work through Example 67, as described above, and try to fill in the gaps.*

- ***Example 70*** *shows a variation from another of J. C. Bach's variation sets. (You will notice that there are problems with the notation of accidentals, which sometimes seem to apply only to the note they immediately precede, as for instance in bar 5; you will have to resolve these problems as best you can.) Try to reconstruct the original theme on which Example 70 is based.*

ASSIGNMENT 31

Using ***Example 71*** *as a theme, write the first half of two variations in J. C. Bach's style, and complete one of them. (Non-keyboard players might prefer to write for string trio, using the second movement of Haydn's Divertimento in A Hob. V: 7 as a model.)*

Ex. 70

Ex. 71 Haydn, Sonata
Hob. XVII: D1,
Minuet

Example 72 shows the theme and four of the eight variations that Mozart based on the chorus 'Dieu d'amour' from Grétry's opera *Les mariages samnites*, together with the first few bars of the remaining four. Mozart wrote this variation set in 1781, only seven years after the publication of Bach's Op. 17. But in Mozart's hands the genre of piano variations has a maturity it lacks in Bach's. The basic difference is that Mozart's variations don't have that tendency towards the mechanical that Bach's sometimes do.

Mozart uses the same study-like figurations as Bach; Variation 2 in Example 72, for instance, is full of conventional, out-of-the-packet patterns. Indeed, if you compare Mozart's different variation sets, you can see that he invents and recycles his own clichés. (Variation 6, in particular, is a pattern that Mozart used over and over again, most illustriously in the A major Sonata, KV 331.) But he uses these patterns much more flexibly than Bach. Variation 2 illustrates this well. If he started a variation like this, Bach would continue the left hand figuration throughout, or at most swap the hands half-way through. Mozart, on the other hand, swaps the hands after two bars, introduces a new pattern based on broken octaves in bar 5, changes hands in bars 9 and again in bar 11, has both hands playing in parallel tenths in bars 13–14, suddenly removes all the figuration at bar 15 to create a little cadenza, and ends the variation as it began, with figuration in the left hand.

Mozart uses the same variation technique he taught Attwood, but in a very free manner. The melody notes of the theme are almost always to be found at the top of the texture in the variations, although they are frequently off the beat and encrusted with ornamentation; Mozart's variations can be so ornate that it becomes a special event when, for once, he quotes the original melody, as in bars 11–12 of Variation 2. This means that Mozart generally retains the melodic contour of the original. The bass notes are usually there in the variations, too, but Mozart sometimes changes the register or inverts the original harmony; bar 2 of Variation 2 illustrates this. Bars 14–15 show that he is also willing to change the harmony on occasion, omitting the inflection towards D minor and approaching the V^{6-5}_{4-3} by a different route. In this way Mozart retains the original melody, bass line, and harmony most of the time, but is prepared to modify any of them when the need rises. The only thing that is completely invariant (at least in this set of variations) is the phrase and cadential structure.

Variations 5 and 7 are special cases. Variation 5 is special because it is in the minor mode; most (but not all) of Mozart's variation sets include a minor-mode variation. Now, any music in the minor will normally transfer quite easily to the major, at least until it begins to modulate; you can test this by playing Variation 5 in F major, adapting the accidentals as you go along. But it is not always so easy the other way round; the problem generally comes from the sixth and seventh degrees of the scale, which may or may not need to be sharpened, depending on the context. Try playing Mozart's theme as if it had a F minor key signature. You have to add or change some accidentals as you play (E♮s in bars 1–4, either B♮s and D♮s or B♭s and D♭s in bar 6, and D♮s in bars 7–8), but basically there is no problem in the first half. Bars 13–14 are more awkward; Mozart changes the harmony extensively at this point in Variation 5. But even this progression *could* be made to work in the minor by means of judiciously chosen accidentals (**Example 73**).

Minor-mode variations are generally doleful, or languorous, or both, and Variation 5 is no exception with its chromatic appoggiaturas in both hands (bars 1 and 5) and

Ex. 72 Mozart, Variations on 'Dieu d'amour', KV 352

Ex. 72 *cont.*

Var. 2

Ex. **72** *cont.*

Var. 7

etc.

Ex. 73

Neapolitan coloration in bar 7. (Classical composers regularly used the Neapolitan sixth, or ♭II^6, as an alternative to ordinary II^6 in II^6–V$^{6-5}_{4-3}$ progressions.) But Variation 7, the Adagio variation, is even more languorous. Again, most of Mozart's variation sets include one such variation, and they are often a great deal longer and more complicated than this one. They are really fantasy-arias, consisting of an extravagantly ornate melodic line in the right hand (thickened at the main cadences), with a relatively simple left-hand part consisting mainly of chords. This one is typical in its profusion of ornamental figures, most of which only last for a bar or two and then disappear: syncopations (bars 6 and 10), triplets (bar 7), running thirty-second notes (bar 11), and trills (bar 14). Typical also is the profusion of chromatic notes and appoggiaturas (the opening bars illustrate this well). The basic principle of the Mozart Adagio variation (and remember that this is a relatively modest example) seems to be that the music hovers constantly on the brink of incoherence, but never *quite* goes over the edge.

Despite the riot of embellishment, the melody line of Variation 7 sticks quite close to that of the theme. But it is not actually modelled on the theme; it is modelled on Variation 1. It elaborates the elaborations in Variation 1, down to the highly operatic cadence figure in bars 11–12. When you compare the two variations, you can see that the elaboration added in Variation 7 is primarily linear: chromatic passing notes are added between diatonic steps, diatonic passing notes are added between thirds, and complete scales are added between larger intervals (bar 7). Or existing scale runs are extended and elaborated (bar 11). Ornamentation of this sort has a long history before Mozart. There are, for instance, a number of performing versions of Corelli's Violin Sonatas in existence, ascribed among others to Geminiani, Tartini, and Corelli himself, which show written-out ornamentation very like that of Variation 7. Figures like those of bars 1 and 12, then, are probably good evidence of the way in which complex turns and other ornaments were performed in the late eighteenth century, even when they weren't written out like this. In this way Mozart's variation technique must have been largely an extension of contemporary performance practice.

Ex. 74 Mozart, *Des kleinen Friedrichs Geburtstag*, KV 529

Ex. 74 *cont.*

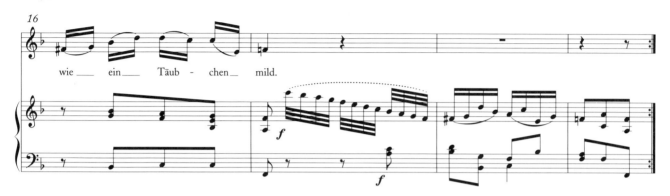

wie ___ ein ___ Täub - chen ___ mild.

ASSIGNMENT 32

This assignment is to be worked at the keyboard, and is in two parts.

- *Play through Example 72, and try to continue the variations of which only the first few bars are given.*
- *Example 74 is 'Des kleinen Friedrichs Geburtstag', written by Mozart in 1787. (The title means 'Little Frederick's birthday' and the Frederick in question was the prince of Anhalt-Dessau.) Turn it into a minor-mode piece by adding an F minor key signature and appropriate accidentals.*

ASSIGNMENT 33

*Arrange **Example 74** as a theme for piano variations, and write the first half of three variations, including a minor-mode one and an Adagio one. Complete at least one of these.*

ASSIGNMENT 34

Choose any set of variations by Mozart and write a short (approximately two-page) analytical commentary on it. Be sure to discuss the theme as well as the variations. Use diagrams where appropriate to clarify your analysis.

CHAPTER 8

The Classic Composer's Workshop

Ex. 75 Mozart,
Minuet from 'Nannerl
Notebook'

IN Chapter 3 I mentioned Heinrich Koch, the Kapellmeister of Rudolstadt, whose composition manual makes extensive use of sixteen-bar minuets and other miniature dances. Leonard Ratner calls the minuet 'the classic composer's workshop', and it's easy to see why. With its clearly articulated structure, it lends itself to adaptation and reformulation, almost in the manner of a child's building blocks. In this chapter we'll explore some of the methods of adaptation and reformulation that Koch set out in his book.

The little Minuet in **Example 75** is taken from the 'Nannerl Notebook', a collection of miniature pieces—of generally doubtful authorship—which Leopold Mozart assembled in 1759 for his daughter Nannerl, who was four years older than her more famous brother. (It wasn't long before Wolfgang was playing Nannerl's pieces; Leopold added a note at the end of the next piece in the collection saying 'Wolfgang learnt these eight minuets when he was 4 years old'—that is, in 1760.) It consists of eighteen bars: eight in the first section or period, and ten in the second. You can see that the second period is, in essence, the same as the first, but with various sections transposed so as to fit in to the larger tonal pattern, and with one of them repeated. Here is the basic structure of the piece (assuming that the B sections begin on the second beat of the bar).

Bar	1	5		9	15
	A	B	:‖:	A	B
Begins	I	I		V	IV
Ends	I	V		I	I

The two B phrases—bars 5:2–8 and 15:2–18—are virtually the same in each period, except that the second B-phrase is transposed up a fourth so that it leads from IV to I, instead of from I to V. The preceding two bars, however, appear at the same pitch in each period. So the pitch relationship between the successive phrases has been altered. The transposition occurs at the junction between the two phrases. Similarly, bars 13:2–14 repeat the previous two bars but at a different transposition; hence the two extra bars in the second period. It's again where one phrase (or, to be more precise, one two-bar segment) joins another that the change is made. And this is the basic principle of this kind of adaptation. When one phrase or segment joins another, it is frequently possible to repeat the first, or to transpose one relative to the other, or both. This opens up a whole range of possibilities, and **Example 76** illustrates some other ways in which you could adapt the first period of Nannerl's Minuet. (The original music is in the third system down; the other systems show alternatives. Play the original where nothing is shown.)

Ex. 76

The first step in adapting music in this way, then, is to locate what might be called the 'break points' between the various phrases of the original music. Writers of Koch's period used the term 'dissection' for this process of dividing up the music in order to reconfigure it in new patterns. How do you determine where the break points fall between segments? 'Generally speaking', writes Koch, 'only feeling can determine . . . the places where resting points occur in the melody' (*Introductory Essay*, p. 3). Maybe that's all that needs to be said. All the same, it is often possible to see what is responsible for the feeling. There may be a rest between one segment and the next. Or there may be a change of register: there are examples of this in bars 3 and 5 of Nannerl's minuet. But the surest indication is the conclusion of a coherent harmonic motion: all the break points in this minuet are marked by a V–I progression.

ASSIGNMENT 35 □

This assignment is in two parts.

- *The two little compositions in the worksheet are taken from the 'London Notebook' and they were composed when Mozart was 7 or 8 years old. (An inscription in Leopold Mozart's hand says they were written by his son; nobody knows how much help he may have had.) Without doing anything except transposing the existing music, adapt them in the following ways:*

    Example (a)
    - *Adapt the first period (up to the double bar) to end in the tonic.*
    - *Adapt the second period to start in the dominant and end as written.*

    Example (b)
    - *Adapt the first period to end in the dominant.*
    - *Adapt the second period to begin in E minor and end as written.*

    Show your adaptations by adding square brackets to the score and stating how the music is to be transposed. In no case is it necessary to make more than two transpositions.

- ***Example 77*** *shows all that exists of another piece from around the same time, again written in Leopold Mozart's hand. (E♭s seem more reasonable than E♮s in bar 7, and a D♭ may be intended in bar 2.) It was presumably intended to have a second half beginning in B♭ and ending in E♭. Construct a second half by using the same materials in the same order as in the first half, transposed as necessary. You need only write two new bars of music: a second-time bar for the first half (treat the last bar of Example 77 as a first-time bar), and the final bar of the second half. Write out the music in full.*

Ex. 77 Mozart, unfinished composition from around 1764

Ex. 77 *cont.*

In his book, Koch says that the reason for studying these little dance forms in such detail is that they are 'representations in miniature of larger compositions' (p. 118). And so, having established the basic idea that you can chop music into segments and reconfigure them in different ways, Koch goes on to show how you can use this technique to expand sixteen-bar minuets into full-size compositions. He sets about this very systematically. He shows how you can turn a four-bar phrase into a five-, six-, or seven-bar one by *augmenting* the note values, adding an *appendix* to the cadence, or both (**Example 78**). He shows how you can extend a phrase by *repeating the cadence*; in bar 4 of **Example 79** the melody cadences on the third of the chord, while in bar 6 it cadences on the root, giving it greater finality. And he shows how you can expand a four-bar phrase from the middle by repeating the second bar (**Example 80**); he illustrates four different types of repetition, which we can call *simple* (*a*), *embellished* (*b*), *inverted* (*c*), and *transposed* (*d*). (A transposed repetition is, of course, a sequence.)

Now Koch shows these techniques in action. He does this by means of a series of examples based on the sixteen-bar minuet shown in **Example 81a**. (If it looks familiar, turn back to Example 35.) He begins by expanding the second half of the minuet. Since its last four bars are a repetition of bars 5–8, with a modified cadence, one obvious means of expansion is to make the minuet end with a complete statement of bars 1–8, (*b*). But this version is not very satisfactory: what is now a four-bar middle section (bars 9–12)

Ex. 78

Ex. 79

Ex. 80

does not really balance the final eight bars, and the tonic harmony of bar I2 is not a good preparation for the return of the opening. Koch's solution (*c*) is to expand the middle section through the *interpolation* of new cadential phrases after bars 9–10 and II–I2; the middle section now ends on V. (Koch makes some minor changes to the tune; they are quite gratuitous, since the tune would have worked perfectly well in its original version, but musically pleasant. Maybe it simply didn't occur to Koch to repeat everything literally, as a present-day writer of textbooks almost certainly would.)

His next version (*d*) expands on the dominant cadence introduced in (*c*). This time

Ex. 8I

Ex. 81 *cont.*

(d)

(e)

(f)

D.C. al fine

he adds a further eight-bar phrase at the beginning of the second half, and this phrase is clearly in the dominant. It is what Koch would call a 'formal modulation', having its own cadence figure. (He cannot resist making further gratuitous changes to the passage that follows, from bar 17.) He then extends this new eight-bar phrase by adding an internal repetition, in bars 17–18 of (*e*), and does the same in the first and last sections of the piece (bars 7–8, 35–6); in each case the repetition is an embellished one. That brings the minuet up to thirty-eight bars. But Koch has not finished yet! His final version (*f*) adds a four-bar interpolation to the final phrase of the first section (bars 9–12), with the last two bars of the interpolation being themselves repeated (bars 13–14), giving an extra six bars in all. This final version looks shorter than the previous one, but that is only because it is notated with a da capo repeat, making the ABA form explicit. Counting the repeat, the minuet is now fifty bars long.

Koch has given all the intermediate versions between the original sixteen-bar minuet and the fully expanded fifty-bar one in order to demonstrate different techniques of expansion one by one. Normally, if composers took a short form and expanded it, they did not write down the intermediate stages—indeed, there probably *were* no intermediate stages, for what Koch sets out is a pedagogical rationale rather than an account of the compositional process. But you can still see what techniques of expansion are involved by setting the original and the expanded versions of the music side by side and comparing the two.

ASSIGNMENT 36 ☐

This assignment is in two parts, and may be combined with the following one.

- *The worksheet shows the original and expanded versions of the first half of another piece from Koch's book. Put brackets round the additions, and indicate at each point the technique of expansion that has been used. You will find all the technical terms you need in the preceding paragraphs.*
- *The worksheet shows the first half of a sonata movement by Haydn (from Hob. XVI: 3). It is possible to see it as a regular sixteen-bar period that has been expanded by means of repetition, varied repetition, and interpolation. Reconstruct the original period by putting brackets round all the expansions. (There are several plausible answers to this question.)*

ASSIGNMENT 37

Choose any minuet from the previous chapters, and write an expanded version of its first half. Your expanded version should be at least 24 bars long.

Because he was a teacher—because he wanted to clarify the principles and techniques of expansion—Koch made his examples a little artificial. On the whole, real composers were more flexible in the way they used expansion techniques. A long piece might be based on a shorter one, but it would not usually proceed from phrase to phrase, expanding each in turn, in the manner of Example 81. Instead, it would use some phrases of the original, expanding these in a number of ways, repeating them, altering their tonal structure, or changing their order; other phrases might be altogether ignored. A more typical example of how techniques of expansion were used, then, is provided by the second

Ex. 82 Theme from Haydn's 'Der Geburtstag', transposed (*a*), and his Symphony No. 14, second movement (*b*)

movement of Haydn's Symphony No. 14, which probably dates from the mid-1760s. This movement is based on the theme from the divertimento 'Der Geburtstag', which featured in Chapter 6. **Example 82a** shows the theme transposed to D major, the key of the symphony movement; this is transcribed in its entirety in (*b*).

The movement opens in the same way as the divertimento theme: the opening is repeated—but embellished in the manner of the final phrase of the theme—and then there is a new cadential pattern, closing on the dominant. (The remainder of the first section, up to the double bar, simply continues in the dominant.) Bars 9–10 of the symphony movement are modelled on—but not identical to—bars 9–10 of the theme; they are repeated sequentially, leading to a phrase that does not come from the theme at all (bars 13–15). At this point there comes the first disturbance of the regular periodic structure: in effect a bar has been missed out between bars 15 and 16. From here to the end of the section there is a succession of closing figures—short, repeated patterns that move strongly towards a cadence point. These closing figures are derived from the theme, in the sense that they employ rhythmic or melodic motives found there (for instance, compare bar 18 of the symphony movement with bar 6 of the divertimento theme). But they do not function in the same way; there are no short, repeated closing figures in the theme.

This means that while materials from the divertimento theme are used in the symphony movement, and while its phrases are expanded by means of the techniques described by Koch, the manner in which this is done is more fluid and informal than in Koch's examples. The divertimento theme and the symphony movement share a binary organization moving from tonic to dominant and back again, but beyond this very general level there is no particular correspondence between the form of the theme and that of the symphony movement as a whole; the second section of the symphony movement (from the double bar to the end) is based on the first section, rather than being based in any direct sense on the divertimento theme. The structure of this second section is obvious enough. Bar 49 corresponds to bar 9; from there to the end, the music is the same as bars 9–27, except that it is transposed to the tonic. As for the beginning of the second section, it consists of . . .

ASSIGNMENT 38

Complete this analysis of Example 82b.

ASSIGNMENT 39

Write the first half of a symphonic movement based on the Mozart theme in Example 65. Model your movement loosely on Example 82b: that means using the same techniques as Haydn, not adhering slavishly to his harmonies or the details of his form. Conceive the music for orchestra rather than for the keyboard, but write it in the form of a two- or occasionally three-part reduction, as in Example 82b.

CHAPTER 9

Cadenzas

'IF a well-written composition can be compared with a noble architectural edifice in which symmetry must predominate,' wrote the early nineteenth-century pianist and pedagogue, Carl Czerny, 'then a fantasy well done is akin to a beautiful English garden, seemingly irregular, but full of surprising variety, and executed rationally, meaningfully, and according to plan.'

There are two fundamentally different organizational principles in Classical music. One is the principle we explored in the last chapter, according to which phrases are repeated, extended, added to other phrases, and so a large piece of music is built up. Cadences punctuate the flow of the music, and the effect is comparable to rhyming verse—or, as Czerny said, to the symmetries of neo-classical architecture. The other, which is the topic of this chapter, is the exact opposite; if Czerny compared it to an English garden (he has something like Stourhead in mind), then we could compare it to musical prose. And an example of the sort of fantasy (or fantasia) that Czerny had in mind is **Example 83**. It was written by Mozart around 1776, and the very handwriting reflects the freedom of the music. As you can see from the transcription in **Example 84**, there are none of the symmetries of the music we've met up to now. There are no phrases and no tunes. There are no bar lines (and hence no metre); there is not even an overall key, since the fantasy begins in F and ends in E minor. Possibly it was intended as an introduction to a fugue in that key.

Despite this freedom, the music is, as Czerny put it, 'executed rationally, meaningfully, and according to plan'. **Example 85** shows the plan: a coherent bass line, with figures. Mozart's fantasy elaborates this plan by means of a series of wave-like melodic gestures (sometimes with waves within waves), made out of arpeggios, arpeggios with appoggiaturas, broken-chord patterns, and diatonic or chromatic scales. The style is improvisatory in the extreme. Indeed music of this sort was usually only written down for pedagogical purposes. C. P. E. Bach gives the bass line for a fantasy, together with a written-out version of it, in his *Essay on the True Art of Playing Keyboard Instruments* (1762); Czerny includes a very similar written-out fantasy in his *Systematic Introduction to Improvisation on the Pianoforte*, published in 1836. Together with Mozart's fantasy, these are among the few remnants of a continuing performance tradition that ran in parallel with the notated works we play today.

As I suggested, this irregular, unmeasured, extemporized music is less like verse than like prose, or even ordinary speech; in fact it is closely related to the *recitativo secco* of Baroque and early Classical opera, which was in effect speech heightened by musical tones. Sophisticated forms of Classical music such as sonata resulted from the interaction of the two musical principles I have described: closed, symmetrical structure based on phrases, and open, irregular *Fortspinnung* based on dramatic gesture. ('Fortspinnung' simply means spinning out; but the English isn't used as a technical term for music, as

Ex. 83 Mozart, Modulating prelude, autograph

Ex. 84 (opposite)

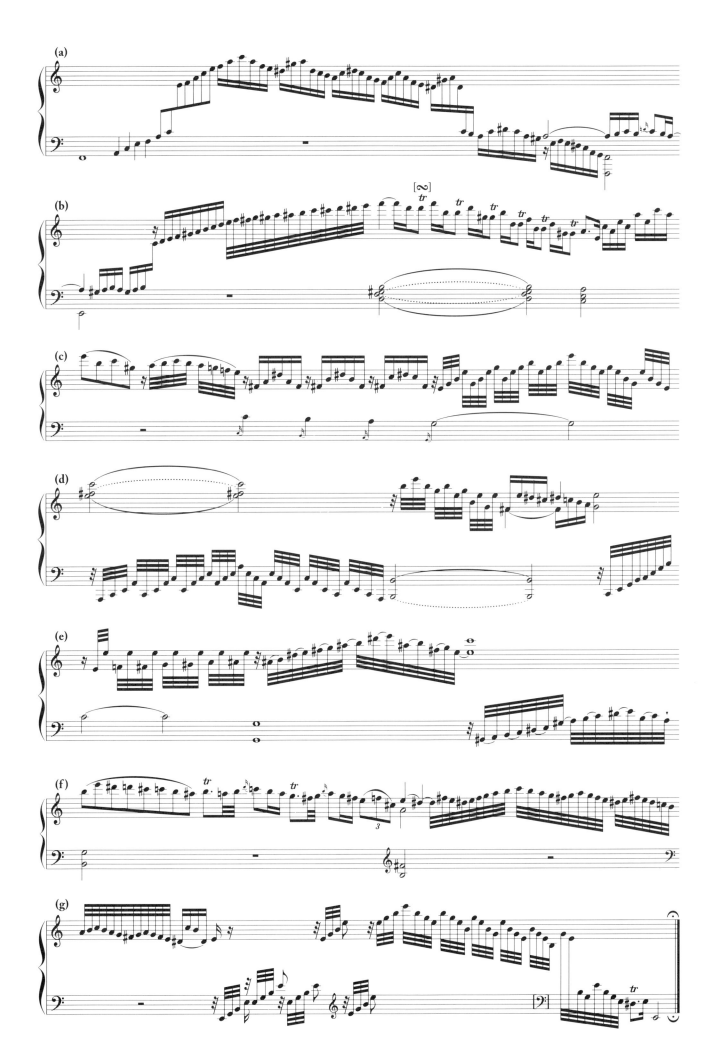

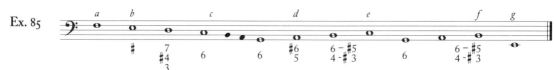

Ex. 85

the German is.) The best way to recapture this aspect of Classical performance practice, and to see how it interacts with the principle of closed, symmetrical structure, is to look at some cadenzas. At its simplest, the cadenza is just a little bit of melodic elaboration at a *fermata*; this is purely an aspect of performance practice. But a fully elaborated Classical cadenza is integrated into the compositional structure of the music. We'll begin with the first and work through to the second.

Properly speaking, cadenzas involve harmonic progressions or modulations to other keys; simple elaborations of a single harmony are known as *Eingänge* (literally, 'entrances'). An example is found in the theme of Mozart's variations on 'Ein Weib ist das herrlichste Ding', KV 613, shown in **Example 86**. (My apologies for the sexist title.

Ex. 86 Mozart, Variations on 'Ein Weib ist das herrlich-ste Ding', KV 613, theme

The composer of the original theme is not known.) This *Eingang* consists of a little melodic arabesque based on the notes of the dominant triad, and marked *a piacere*, which means the same as 'ad lib'. Then, in each subsequent variation, Mozart writes out an *Eingang* adapted to the character of the individual variation. These are shown (together with the preceding bar) in **Example 87**. Each *Eingang* adds between one and four bars to the length of the music and prolongs a C major chord; the C major chord begins as a temporary tonic and ends as a V of F major. As with the fantasy in Examples 83–4, the elaborations consist of arpeggios (simple arpeggios in Variations 2 and 7, broken ones in Variations 3 and 4); arpeggios with appoggiaturas (Variation 1, bar 2 of the *Eingang*); and diatonic or chromatic scales, normally connecting harmony notes of the V or V⁷ chord, and sometimes elaborated by means of neighbour notes (Variations 1, 2, 3, 5, and 7).

Ex. 87 Mozart, variations on 'Ein Weib ist das herrlichste Ding', *Eingänge*

Ex. 87 *cont.*

There are occasional touches of other harmonies: in bar 2 of the *Eingang* from Varation 7, V^7 alternates with a minor-inflected II^7, while in the preceding F minor variation the V^7 at the same point is initially replaced by a diminished seventh chord. But these harmonies do not create harmonic rhythm or phrase structure; even the II^7–V^7 alternations of Variation 7 create at most a little island of regularity surrounded by metrical freedom. In the same way, the texture of the *Eingänge* is fairly varied, ranging from a single melodic line in one or the other hand, through a chordally supported melody line (Variations 5 and 7), to octaves (Variation 3). But there is no counterpoint. These *Eingänge* are in essence vocal **melismas** transcribed for keyboard. Their basic structure can be described in the simplest of analytical terms: high versus low, fast versus slow, tense versus relaxed.

The *Eingänge* of KV 613 use the prevailing note values of the variation in which they are located and, except in the case of the final flourish of the *Eingang* in Variation 7, they connect registrally with what precedes and follows them. But they don't use the same melodic motifs as what comes before (otherwise there might be no sense of a fermata), and only in Variation 4 does the left hand figuration continue without a break at the beginning of the *Eingang*. On the other hand, several of the *Eingänge* lead without a break into the ensuing section of the variation, as in Variations 2, 4, and 5.

The *Eingang* of Variation 7 is the only one which falls into more or less distinct sections; it is the one that comes closest to being a true cadenza.

ASSIGNMENT 40

Example 88 shows the theme and part of four variations from Mozart's 'Lison dormait' variations, KV 264 (based on an opera by Nicolas Dezède). Just as in KV 613, there is a fermata on the dominant in the second half (bar 16). This time, however, Mozart has supplied only the most rudimentary indications for Eingänge, and in some cases nothing at all. But it would be perfectly in style for there to be more extended Eingänge at these points, and a contemporary performer would very likely have improvised them. Supply Eingänge for the theme and the four variations in Example 88, giving each Eingang a distinct character and matching it to the mood and rhythmic value of the variation. There is no need to incorporate Mozart's rudimentary Eingänge.

Ex. 88 Mozart, Variations on 'Lison dormait', KV 264

Thema

Ex. 88 *cont.*

Var. 2, bars 9–24

Var. 5, bars 9–25

Var. 6, bars 9–24

Var. 7, bars 9–24

It's usual to associate cadenzas with concertos. But there are cadenzas in solo pieces too. Some of Mozart's piano variations include a full-blown cadenza as well as *Eingänge*; the cadenza comes towards the end of the final variation, bringing the entire set of variations to a climax. **Example 89** shows the final variation, including a cadenza, from KV 264.

Ex. 89 Mozart, Variations on 'Lison dormait', final variation

Var.9

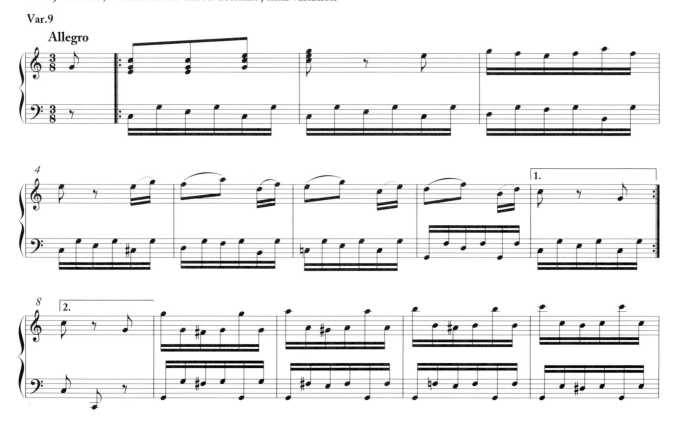

Ex. 89 *cont.*

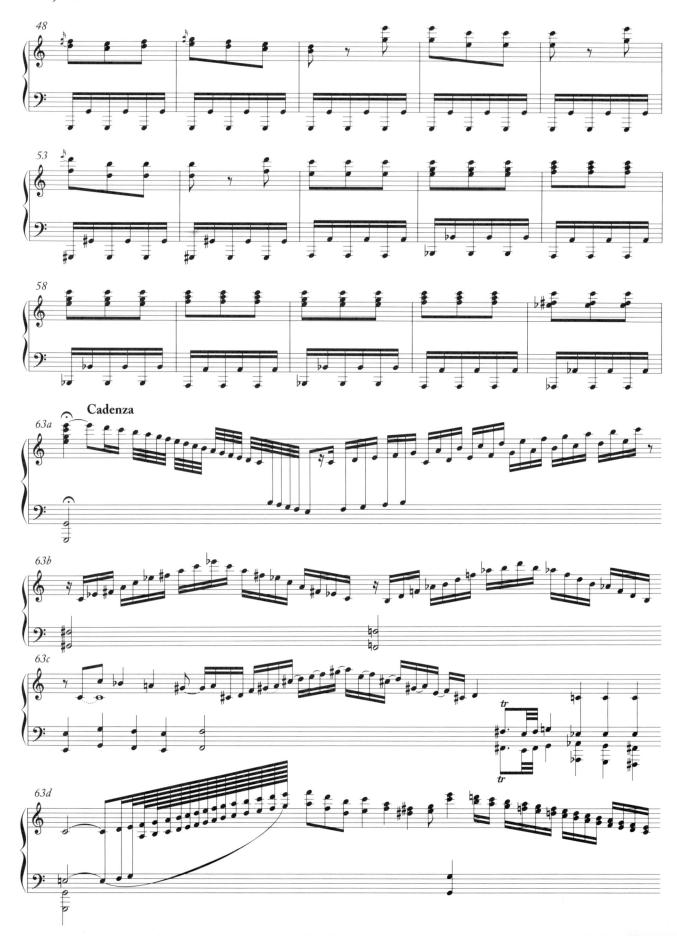

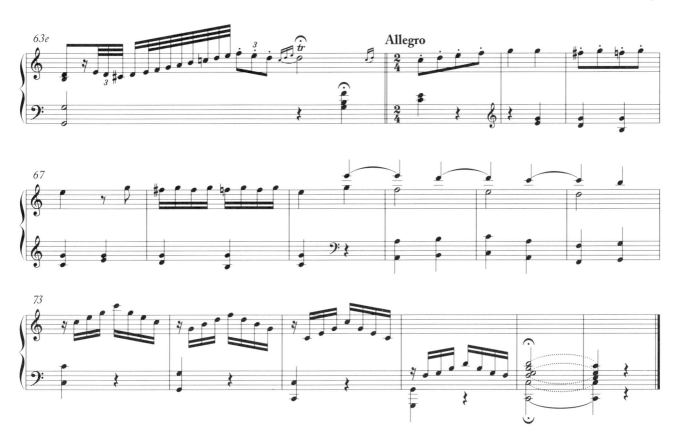

If an *Eingang* prolongs a V, then a cadenza prolongs a V^{6-5}_{4-3}. **Example 90** shows how this applies to the cadenza in Example 89 as a whole. This reduction works in essentially the same way as those in earlier chapters, for instance Example 34. That is to say, it picks out the most important notes, showing how they connect with one another to form coherent harmonic and linear motions. But it is dealing with considerably more complicated music than the earlier reductions, and for this reason the analysis is separated into two systems: (*b*) is a reduction of (*a*), just as (*a*) is a reduction of Mozart's cadenza.

As you can see, the use of slurs comes into its own in this analysis. As always, they are used to show groups of notes that belong together. Most obviously, they are used in (*a*) to mark the outer limits of the scales and arpeggios that surge up and down the keyboard. Similarly, they link together the notes of the D minor arpeggio in bar 63[c] (the appoggiaturas of the original are of course omitted), and the patterns of falling thirds in bar 63[d]. But there is a more subtle principle at work, and this can be seen by comparing Example 90*a* and *b*. Each of the notes that appears in (*a*) but not in (*b*) is linked by a slur to a note that *does* appear in (*b*); in this way the slurs show exactly how (*a*) relates to (*b*). Moreover, the same principle applies to the slurs at (*b*); these relate the notes there to the structural harmonies represented by the Roman letters. (Every note that appears in (*b*) but doesn't belong to a structural harmony is linked by a slur to a note that does.) The principle, then, is that slurs show how groups of notes at any given level correspond to single notes or chords at the next level. Finally, tails are added to the most important notes of all in (*b*)—those that outline the V^{6-5}_{4-3} progression on which the entire cadenza is based.

Making an analysis of this kind is quite an intricate process. But it's not too hard to understand what it is saying. The essential plan of the whole cadenza is the bass line in

Ex. 90

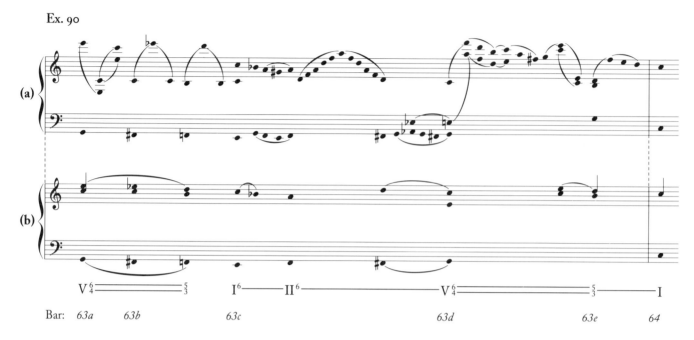

Example 90*b*, which fulfils much the same role as the bass line in Example 85; it moves from G down to E and up to G again, with the two Gs supporting V$^6_4$ harmonies, the second of which resolves to $^5_3$. The upper stave of (*b*) shows the counterpoint with this bass line that underlies the cadenza. All the notes in the upper stave of (*b*) appear in (*a*), but there is a tremendous amount of registral displacement. The slurs show the leaps of two octaves or more that are opened up by these displacements and which, in the actual cadenza, are filled by the now familiar means—arpeggios, arpeggios with appoggiaturas, scales, and so on. The essential wave-like pattern of an *Eingang* is still there, but instead of appearing on the surface it has been composed deep into the structure of the music.

There is more to a cadenza then what is marked 'Cadenza' in the music. Equally important is the way in which it is approached. In Example 89, the variation proceeds normally until bar 53, except that the repeat of the second half is written out in full, with the disposition of the hands being reversed from bar 41 on. But in bar 53—just six bars from what would be the end of the variation—the bass rises to G♯. This echoes bar 29, where the bass also rose to G♯, initiating a VI–IV–V–I cadential progression that completed itself within the established phrase structure. In bars 53–62, however, the G♯ rises through A to B♭, before falling chromatically back to G. Although it is easy enough to assign Roman letters to the chords supported by this bass line, the progression is not really a harmonic one at all: you can test this by playing all the chords in root position. The continuity of the music comes not from the chords as such—and certainly not from the melody, because that disappears after bar 54—but from the linear motion of the bass.

The descending bass creates a sense of motion towards the V on which the cadenza is built, and the feeling of arrival is heightened by the ♭VI$^{\#6}$ of the previous bar—one

Ex. 91

of the standard approaches to the cadential $^6_4$. (**Example 91** shows several such approaches.) But this is not the kind of measured motion that creates regular phrase structure. Without a clearly articulated chord progression, without a regular sequence of upbeats and downbeats, the phrase structure of the music dissipates. This is easy to test, too: you can omit bars 60–1 without disrupting the musical structure in the way that an eight-bar phrase is disrupted when two bars are cut out of it. To be sure, doing this diminishes the effect of prolongation, of postponing the moment of resolution. But this is simply a function of the passing of time. When there is no sense of phrase structure, musical time becomes indistinguishable from everyday time. Bars 41–62 of Example 89 constitute a kind of modulation from structured, musical time—what we could call compositional time—to the real time of performance. The effect is that the performer, who has up to this point functioned primarily as a medium for the transmission of the work, comes to stage centre. These bars, then, form a transition from composition to improvisation—even though Mozart has written out the music to be 'improvised'.

The final element of Example 89 that needs to be looked at is the coda, from bar 64 to the end. Mozart's procedure here is typical: he begins what appears to be a further variation, closely related to the opening theme. Bars 68–9 are a varied repeat of 66–7, just as bars 5–6 are a varied repeat of 3–4. But thereafter the scheme is disrupted. Bars 70–1 are, in effect, a further repetition of these bars (the F–E in the inner part makes this plain). The fragmentation of phrase structure that arises from this—always a sign that the music is moving towards a point of climax or conclusion—is underlined by a rhythmic *elision* at bar 73, which functions both as the end of one phrase (bars 70–3) and the beginning of the next (bars 73–8). This last phrase of the music consists of nothing but I and V harmonies supporting the most stereotyped melodic material. The sense of a conclusion arises from the reduction of the music to harmonic essentials, and the repetition of brief fragments from which all characteristic thematic content has been eliminated (a process sometimes termed *liquidation*).

Although the cadenza of KV 264 incorporates contrasted sections, structural counterpoint, and chord progressions within the overall V^{6-5}_{4-3} framework, there is one feature

Ex. 92 Mozart, Variations on 'Les hommes pieusement', KV 455, theme (*a*) and final variation (*b*)

(a)

Ex. 92 *cont.*

(b)   **Var. 10**
       Allegro

Ex. 92 *cont.*

Ex. 92 *cont.*

of the most fully developed cadenza that it lacks. This is thematic reference. There is nothing to link the cadenza of KV 264 to the theme. In fact there is no very obvious reason why the cadenza of KV 264 could not be transplanted to any other set of variations in C major. But this is not true of Mozart's variations on Gluck's 'Les hommes pieusement' (from the opera *La rencontre imprévue*), KV 455, the theme (*a*) and final variation (*b*) of which are shown in **Example 92**. Whereas the first and last sections of the cadenza (bars 52–7 and 95–112 of (*b*)) are made up of entirely anonymous patterns of figuration, the middle section (bars 58–94) is based on the theme, or more precisely it is based on the final variation.

Bar 58 serves as an introduction. This is followed by a pair of regular eight-bar phrases, in which a variant of bars 1–4 appears first in the tonic, and then in the tonic minor. Then, in bars 75–8, the eight-bar pattern is broken down into a four-bar one, still in tonic minor. Then this is repeated in sequence, each time a third lower (G minor, E♭ major, C minor). Nothing could be more different from the irregularity and freedom of the KV 264 cadenza; these bars of the KV 455 cadenza are regular to the point of being mechanical. But that is just the point. The music starts to repeat itself, rambling on and losing any sense of direction. The four-bar phrases are still there on the surface of the music, but they do not fit together into any larger pattern. The V–I motions are still there, but they are going nowhere. The thematic reference is still there, but repetition has rendered it banal and meaningless. And from bar 86, the theme disintegrates into arpeggio figuration, while the harmonic progression slips from C minor, through A♭ major, to the muddy-sounding diminished sevenths of bars 90–4. Any residual sense of phrasing evaporates. Then the diminished harmony is suddenly reinterpreted as V^7, and the final section of the cadenza begins.

What is the effect of the middle section of this cadenza? It is one of recollection; the music from the beginning of the variation appears as if it were in quotation marks.

ASSIGNMENT 41

Write an analytical essay on the whole of the finale of KV 455 (Example 92b), illustrated where appropriate by diagrams or reductions.

ASSIGNMENT 42

Example 93 *shows the Theme and Variation 2 of Mozart's KV 460, based on the aria 'Come un agnello' from Giuseppe Sarti's opera Fra i due litiganti. Mozart wrote this in 1784 (the same year as KV 455), but never completed the work: all that exists is the theme and two variations. Adapt Variation 2 in such a way as to turn it into a full-scale finale for a variation set, loosely modelling it on Example 92b. (Imagine that there are five or six variations coming before it.) This means:*

- *Writing out the repeat of bars 9–16, possibly with some minor changes. (This corresponds to bars 9–24 in Example 92b.)*
- *Altering the repeat of bars 17–24 in such a way that, instead of coming to a close, the music continues to a V^6_4, ready for the cadenza. (This corresponds to bars 25–51 in Example 92b.)*
- *Adding a cadenza, incorporating thematic elements and different keys.*
- *Adding a coda modelled on the opening of the theme. (This corresponds to bars 113–33 in Example 92b.)*

Ex. 93 Mozart, Variations on 'Come un agnello'

Thema

Ex. 93 *cont.*

Var. 2

Part IV

Sonata

Introduction to Part IV

THE purpose of this final part is to show how the different techniques and principles I've described work together to create sustained and highly organized compositional structures. So it takes the form of a series of case studies. The choice of piano music was dictated by practicality and convenience. The choice of sonata first movements, by contrast, was a more or less inevitable consequence of the special place that the sonata occupies within the Classical style.

The sonata, or rather the idea of the sonata, has a curious history. In its origin, the word simply means something sounded, that is to say something to be played by instruments (as opposed to 'cantata', which means something to be sung). By the Classical period, the meaning of the term had narrowed to a composition in several movements for a solo instrument, with or without accompaniment (piano sonata, violin sonata, and so on). Late eighteenth-century theorists never gave a fixed, prescriptive account of what a sonata was like; they merely said things like how many movements sonatas were *usually* in, patterns into which their first movements *tended to* fall, and so on.

Theorists like Koch were writing for interested amateurs who wanted to deepen their knowledge of music and (what was seen as in effect the same thing) to develop their skills in composition. This is what sets the tone of Koch's composition manual: friendly, descriptive, and practical. By the middle of the nineteenth century, however, composition manuals were beginning to be designed for a quite different readership. This was largely the result of the institutionalization of music education: instead of working as performers and perhaps taking private lessons, like Attwood, budding composers increasingly enrolled in a conservatory. (Since he was one of the Royal Academy of Music's first professors, as I mentioned, Attwood's career neatly summarizes this transition.) There they took more or less fixed courses, and used textbooks which prescribed the form of their studies. And these textbooks included, among other things, blueprints of the historical forms which apprentice composers were expected to adopt in their own music. Among these pride of place was given to what now became known as 'sonata form' (a term unknown to the Classical composers, and first used around 1840 by Adolf Bernhard Marx).

Because they were directed towards students, these nineteenth-century composition manuals had an altogether different tone from Koch's: they tended to be less friendly and more formal. And they were prescriptive rather than descriptive, saying not what generally was done but what *ought* to be done. They represented the Classical sonata as a recipe, a set of rules to be followed more or less unthinkingly. And they led people to try and understand Classical music by reading textbooks rather than by going to the music itself. In this context analysis became little more than an exercise in trying to fit existing pieces of music into the patterns prescribed by the textbooks. As a result, it gained a reputation for being divorced from practice; it was seen as being academic in the bad sense. Some people still see analysis that way.

The twentieth century has seen a massive backtracking from this prescriptive concept of sonata form. We still talk about sonata form, but we are no longer quite comfortable with the term. We are happier talking about the sonata 'principle'; the American pianist and theorist Charles Rosen has even gone so far as to refer to 'a texture called the sonata'. It is Rosen, more than anyone, who has set the terms within which most people think of sonata today. The title of one of his books states his basic message in two words: *Sonata Forms*. For Rosen, there is a basic conception of music, a shaping principle, that defines the Classical sonata. Essentially this means seeing a piece of music as an imaginary drama of conflict and reconciliation, realized through theme and key. (You could say that a movement in sonata form is in effect an operatic scene in which the characters have been replaced by themes and keys, and the stage by the listener's imagination.) And this concept of music as drama can be realized in any number of different ways. Looked at in a moment-to-moment manner, that is to say in terms of the musical surface, Classical sonatas offer a bewildering range of forms: there is no such thing as 'sonata form' in the textbook sense.

Chapters 10 and 11, then, attempt to outline the sonata principle through comparative study of a number of different sonata forms. One of the assignments involves a further comparison: between a Mozart sonata movement in its finished state, and a draft of it that Mozart discarded during the compositional process. This is of more than antiquarian interest; seeing what a composer *didn't* want—what he considered inadequate—can help us to understand what he *did* want, and why. (Incidentally I'm not going to make a pretence of equal opportunities in Classical music, by saying 'what he or she considered inadequate'. Classical music was the product of a substantially male-dominated society; it was almost exclusively composed by men, though frequently performed by women.) And that leads to the final chapter, which follows the stages through which Beethoven composed one of his most familiar piano works, the little Sonata in G major, Op. 49 No. 2.

Further reading

- Charles Rosen's key work is *The Classical Style: Haydn, Mozart, Beethoven* (London and New York, 1971; revised edition, 1976).
- In Chapter 11 I briefly refer to the idea of 'topics' in Classical music. A general account may be found in Chapter 2 of Leonard Ratner's *Classic Music: Expression, Form, and Style*; he has also written a short article specifically about the first movement of Mozart's KV 284 ('Topical Content in Mozart's Keyboard Sonatas', *Early Music*, 19 (1991), 615–19), from which the analysis on p. 182 below is taken.
- The same issue of *Early Music* also contains a study of Mozart's revision of the first movement of KV 284: László Somfai's 'Mozart's First Thoughts: The Two Versions of the Sonata in D Major, K. 284' (601–13).
- The account of the sonata offered in these chapters has been designed to link in with Chapter 8 of my *Guide to Musical Analysis* (London and New York, 1987), which offers among other things a more detailed account of Beethoven's Op. 49 No. 2.
- Chapter 12 includes extracts from the 'Kafka Miscellany'. Edited and transcribed by Joseph Kerman, this is published under the title *Ludwig van Beethoven: Autograph Miscellany from circa 1786 to 1799* (2 vols., London, 1970).
- The most approachable introduction to Beethoven's sketches and the compositional process is still Alan Tyson's 'Sketches and Autographs', in Denis Arnold and Nigel Fortune (eds.), *The Beethoven Companion* (London, 1971), 443–58. The field has however developed considerably since then, largely as a result of Tyson's own work; for more up-to-date references see Barry Cooper *et al.*, *The Beethoven Compendium* (London, 1991).

CHAPTER 10

The Complementation of Dance and Fantasy

THE Classical sonata was a style of synthesis. As Leonard Ratner puts it, 'In sonata form, dance and fantasia complement each other; periods begin as dances but often move to the fantasia by means of digressions and extensions, to return to the dance at the beginning of the next period. . . . These are worked together so deftly that neither controls the other.' (*Classic Music*, p. 233). Perhaps the best way to understand what Ratner means is to look at an early Classical movement that is, in essence, an expanded binary dance, but in which certain fantasy-like elements nevertheless play an essential part.

Example 94 shows the first movement of J. C. Bach's Sonata Op. 5 No. 3. Its first eight bars form a regular, closed unit, much like the first half of a sixteen-bar dance (or perhaps one of Mozart's songs). Melodically there is a complex arch contour, and harmonically the whole eight bars are tied together by the I . . . I⁶–IV–V–I progression. All you can really do after something like this is repeat it, and that's what Bach does. But after

Ex. 94 J. C. Bach, Sonata Op. 5 No. 3, first movement

Ex. 94 *cont.*

Ex. 94 *cont.*

two bars he begins to change the harmony. The C♮s become C♯s, pushing the music towards the dominant, D major. There are even inflections towards A major, before the music settles down in D major with a I–II⁶–V cadence (bars 14–16). There is still an eight-bar patterning in the music; bars 9–16 form a kind of unit, corresponding to bars 1–8. But it is a very different sort of unit. Instead of being closed, it moves from I to V of V. It opens up the musical form, demanding an extensive continuation. What begins as a dance form, then, turns into something more open and ongoing.

Bar 17 marks a decisive point of arrival. Historically, there is nothing new in the idea of music going to the dominant: Baroque music constantly did so. What is characteristic of the Classical sonata is that it turns the arrival at the dominant into an *event*. You can see this both in the way the music relaxes after the tensional highpoint of bar 15, and in the introduction of a new and characteristic figure at bar 17. This is the point where a more fully-fledged sonata form would have a second **subject**, a more or less closed melody to mark the dominant. In other words it would revert to the dance-like quality of the opening. Bach does not do this; his figure lasts only two bars and is immediately repeated. But it outlines a V–I motion in D major, and so represents an area of stability. It reinforces the sense of D major being a tonic for the time being; in twentieth-century jargon, it *tonicizes* it.

The remaining material up to the double bar line consists of a succession of short phrases, none more than two bars long, that revolve in diminishing circles round D major; we can call them *closing* figures. They all have the same purpose: to prepare for and dramatize the approaching cadence in the new key. They achieve this in different ways. Bars 21–4 are constructed over a bass line that circles round the A on which it arrives at bar 25. The next two bars (25–6) form a little cadenza, complete with cadential trill. And bars 27–32 crown the final cadence with new, tonic-hugging figures.

Mathematically, it all adds up: 32 bars equals 4 × 8. But is this a musical as well as a mathematical symmetry? Maybe the music retains the traces of regular phrase construction: *something* important happens at bars 1, 9, 17, and 25. But the open, ongoing tonal structure of much of this music means that the underlying symmetry is neither obvious nor important. Bach's opening section could perfectly well have been 30 bars long, or 34, or 35. Plenty of other examples are.

In charting the interaction of dance and fantasia in this movement, we have been differentiating between two basically different types of music: closed and open. Nowadays we use the term *thematic* for the closed, relatively dance-like sections, and terms like *transitional* and *developmental* for the open, relatively fantasy-like sections. And we talk about sonata form being based on the contrast of two themes or subjects, or two thematic or subject areas—represented in Bach's movement by the sections based on G major and D major respectively. Now late eighteenth-century musicians wouldn't have understood this at all; they used the word 'theme' in rather the way that we talk about a speech having a theme, so the idea of a sonata being based on two themes would have struck them as quite odd. Even if it is anachronistic, however, this concept of sonata form being based on oppositions of theme and key is useful, because it gives us a basic framework for analysis. It means that we can think of any Classical movement in sonata form (which includes the first movements of practically all sonatas, and sometimes other movements as well) as being organized round four *thematic events*, coordinated with the key structure:

Theme	A . . .	B . . .	:‖:	A . . .	B . . .
Key	1 . . .	2		X . . .	1

The area of uncertainty, as you can see, is the key associated with the return of the opening theme—the third thematic event, which (following Ratner) I've marked with an 'X'. Although many different formal patterns are found in sonatas, they fall into two broad categories, according to whether the first or the second key is used at this point. As a general rule (but one with lots of exceptions), earlier Classical composers used the second key, while later Classical composers used the first. And as you'll see, a lot turns on this choice.

Bach begins the second half of his movement by repeating the opening theme in the second key, D major. That constitutes the third thematic event. In terms of the basic framework of sonata form, then, all that remains is the final event, the return of the second thematic figure in the first key, G major. This happens something over half-way through the second half of the piece (bar 66). In fact, in terms of the basic plan, the second half of Bach's movement is simply a repeat of the first half, only with the keys reversed:

Bar	1	17		33	66
Theme	A . . .	B . . .	:‖:	A . . .	B . . .
Key	G . . .	D		D . . .	G

Yet that's not, in itself, a very adequate description of what happens; you can see this simply from the fact that the second half is a lot longer than the first (49 bars as against 32). The reason for the discrepancy is that Bach works out this basic plan in terms of the dramatic conception of key that we saw in the first half of the piece. So, although he begins the second half in D major, he doesn't simply let it lead smoothly to G major through a V–I relationship; that wouldn't create the required sense of tonal drama. Instead, he has the music wander away from D major through obliquely related keys such as E minor and B minor. He makes it lose its sense of tonal direction. This way, the return to G major can be projected as a dramatic achievement, a real event, and not just a routine occurrence.

Music that wanders through different keys usually works rather like the Mozart fantasy in Example 83: it is supported by a coherent bass line that moves mainly by step. **Example 95** picks out the most important notes from the bass during bars 41–62, and shows how the passage consists essentially of three stages: first, a mainly scalar ascent to the B at bar 48; second, a prolongation of the B; and third, a cycle of fifths that begins with the B at bar 57, and leads to the G at bar 61. Although the music is constantly moving during bars 40–56, there is no overall sense of where it is moving *from* or *to*. There is no clear sense of tonal implication, hence no clear sense of upbeat and downbeat, and hence no clear phrase structure; even mathematics doesn't reveal eight-bar phrases this time.

Ex. 95

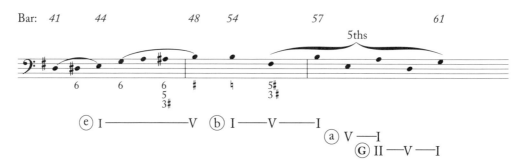

But all this changes during the final approach to G major, in bars 57–61. The sense of regular phrase structure returns; it does so because the music moves through a series of fifths, B–E–A–D–G, the last three of these making up a II–V–I cadence back into the opening key. (Such cycles of fifths, in effect a series of dominant-tonic relationships, create a strong sense of tonal momentum, and are one of the commonest strategies that Classical composers used to underline the return to the overall tonic.) And yet the drama isn't quite over. The music lands on G at bar 61, but it is more like grounding on a sandbar than a controlled, intentional landfall. For a few bars (61–5) the music noodles: it loses its sense of direction, and the regular phrase structure evaporates. Like a cadenza, but in a quite different way, this passage resembles a fermata that has been composed into the musical structure. And its effect is to heighten the drama, the sense of event, when bar 66 appears almost without warning, bringing with it the return of clear tonal direction and regular phrase structure.

Sonata form can seem terribly arbitrary when it is presented in the form of a formula or a recipe. To some extent it *is* arbitrary: composers did things in certain ways because that's how things were done, or how they were taught to do them, and so traditions like sonata form grew up. Nevertheless, once you have grasped the conventions within which Bach is working, most of what he does becomes plain common sense. He begins the second half of his movement by repeating the opening material in the second key, but stops repeating it at the point when it would be moving towards the dominant (bar 42). Instead, he interpolates a lengthy section of new music, freely borrowing materials from the first half of the piece, but moving through a variety of keys without cadencing strongly in any of them. He is aiming for the overall tonic, G major, in which key he will repeat the B-section of the music virtually unchanged (bars 66–81). These are the conventions of the form he has adopted. Within these conventions, he works freely and everything that he does can be understood on its own terms.

ASSIGNMENT 43

This assignment is in two parts.

- Here is a tabular analysis of the first section of Example 94 (in which the 'C' label stands for 'closing'):

Bar				
1	G:	*I*	A	Syncopated cadences
9		*I*		V of V colorations
	=D:	*IV . . . II–V*	A (mod.)	
17		*V–I . . . V*	B	Phrase extension
				Cadential trill (bar 26)
27		*I–V*	C¹	Closing materials
31		*I–V–I*	C²	

[Repeat]

Complete the analysis, and draw a box round any passages in the second half that are not directly derived from the corresponding passage in the first half. Comment on any noteworthy features.

- ***Example 96*** shows the first half of a movement from a Sonatina written in 1796 by another of Mozart's pupils, Anton Eberl. The movement has the same basic form as the first movement of J. C. Bach's Op. 5 No. 3. Try to reconstruct the second half (which is 46 bars long in the original). Here are some notes to help you.

  - Begin by working out the passages derived directly from the first half. The opening of the second half will be the same as the opening of the first half, transposed from I to V; the end of the second half will be the same as the end of the first half, transposed from V to I.

  - Now fill in the gap in the middle. You will probably need to write around fifteen bars of new music. (This will be the equivalent of the passage round which you drew a box in your analysis of Example 94.) Plan out the way you are going to lead back to the tonic, and try to support the tonal motion by means of a coherent bass line.

  - There is no need to write out all the music that is simply transposed from the first half, but you should say whether it is to be transposed up or down.

ASSIGNMENT 44

Example 97 shows a sonata opening that Mozart sketched around 1771. This is probably about the time that he turned some of J. C. Bach's sonatas into concertos, and the style of this fragment is very similar to Bach's. Complete the movement on the model of the first movement of Bach's Op. 5 No. 3.

Ex. 96 Eberl, sonatina movement, first part

Ex. 96 *cont.*

Ex. 97 Mozart, unfinished sonata movement

Ex. 97 *cont.*

CHAPTER 11

Three Into Two Will Go

IN the last chapter I said that the two main categories of sonata form revolved round the key you used for the repeat of the opening material in the second half of the movement. In his Op. 5 No. 3, J. C. Bach used the second key, returning to the first key for the repeat of the opening idea; the result was that the second half of the movement was essentially like the first half, only with the keys reversed. The form is in essence symmetrical:

Theme	A ...		B ...	:‖:	A ...		B ...
Key	1 ...		2		2 ...		1

Now late eighteenth-century writers like Koch did not talk about 'sonata form' (that term was not coined until the middle of the nineteenth century), but they did describe the forms that the first movements of sonatas took. They invariably described them as falling into two halves. But they were generally not very specific about details, particularly as regards the second half. Koch says little more than that the second half may or may not begin with the opening idea in the key of the dominant, and that it ends like the first half only in the tonic.

If the second half begins with the opening idea in the key of the dominant, then we have the form that Bach used in his Op. 5 No. 3. But what if it doesn't? Since Koch supplies so little information, we have to look at what composers did. It's clear that, in the last decades of the eighteenth century, composers increasingly didn't begin the second halves of their sonata first movements with the opening idea in the key of the dominant. But it's hard to say what they *did* do, other than that they used just about any material and in just about any key. (No wonder Koch didn't know what to say!) But, as usual with Classical music, there is a principle at work. And the principle is that, whatever else this initial section of the second half may do, it will end on the dominant, and lead to a repetition of the first half of the movement *with both the A section and the B section in the tonic*. The overall form, then, is like this:

Theme	A ...	B ...	:‖:	New section	A ...	B ...
Key	1 ...	2		... V of	1 ...	1

Why are both the A section and the B section in the tonic? The answer lies in the dramatic conception of musical structure, and particularly of tonal structure, that lies at the heart of sonata. The most convincing account of this conception (an account based on analysing music rather than on period theory) has come from Charles Rosen. He describes large-scale tonal structure in terms of consonance and dissonance, transferring these terms from the note-to-note level to that of large-scale form. The modulation from Key 1 to Key 2 in the first half of a sonata movement, he explains, creates an effect of formal dissonance: it requires resolution, just like a dominant seventh or a suspension. And at the formal level, resolution means restating the essential material of the movement in Key 1, the tonic. In this way, the final A . . . B . . . section doesn't simply balance the first one, like the two halves of a sixteen–bar minuet; it represents the culmination of a process initiated in the first half of the movement.

What, then, is the role of the new section at the beginning of the second half? Its function is to throw the maximum dramatic weight on to the beginning of the final A . . . B . . . section; this point of double return (to the original key and to the opening thematic material) becomes the fulcrum of the entire movement. In effect, then, the new section is a fermata that has been composed into the music on the largest possible scale. It is like a massive cadenza that has become an integral part of the movement. And seen this way, there is no reason to be surprised by the lack of conformity between different composers in the thematic and tonal organization of this section; its only obligatory function is the dominant on which it ends. Apart from that it is pure prolongation and anything goes.

In seeing this first movement sonata form as made up of two halves, theorists like Koch played down the significance of the new section. If this was a tenable point of view as regards Haydn's and Mozart's sonata movements, it had ceased to be so by the time of Beethoven's 'Eroica' Symphony, in which the new section is as substantial as the A . . . B . . . ones. So nineteenth-century theorists, who based their view of sonata on Beethoven, relabelled the form so that it consisted of three equally important parts. And this gave rise to the familiar sonata form of the textbooks, with its *exposition*, *development*, and *recapitulation*:

	Exposition			*Development*	*Recapitulation*	
Theme	A . . .	B . . .	:‖: . . .		A . . .	B . . .
Key	1 . . .	2	. . . .	V of	1 . . .	1

Who were right: the eighteenth- or the nineteenth-century theorists? Is sonata form really binary or ternary? These are not very profitable questions. Naturally the eighteenth-century conception tends to apply better to eighteenth-century music, and the nineteenth-century one to nineteenth-century music. But any sonata has *both* binary *and* ternary aspects, and so neither conception has a monopoly on the truth. Nowadays it is quite usual to use the nineteenth-century terminology of exposition, development, and recapitulation to describe eighteenth-century music, and to be sure this is an anachronism. But then so is using Roman letters to describe Classical music, for the Roman-letter system of harmonic analysis also dates from the nineteenth century.

There is however one respect in which nineteenth-century theory led to a drastic misunderstanding of the Classical sonata. This had to do not with the three-part plan, but with the way it was used. Highly elaborate versions of this plan (with each section subdivided and labelled 'bridge section', 'transition', 'retransition', and so forth) appeared in composition textbooks and in the composition curricula of the newly emerging conservatories of music. Students were required to follow the plan literally and any deviation was marked incorrect. In this way sonata form (as it now began to be called) was seen as a prescription, a set of instructions to be followed to the letter.

Nothing could be more contrary to the idea of sonata as it was understood by the Classical composers. For them it was not a set of instructions but a guiding principle that could result in any number of different musical realizations. And the best way to demonstrate this is to compare two movements which, in one sense, are very similar—they are both by Mozart, and were composed within a year of each other—but which realize the sonata principle in very different ways. These are the first movements of KV 279 (**Example 98**) and KV 284 (**Example 99**), and they were composed in 1774 and 1775

Ex. 98 Mozart, Sonata KV 279, first movement

Sonata

Ex. 98 *cont.*

Ex. 98 *cont.*

Ex. 98 *cont.*

respectively. Both movements are marked 'Allegro' and begin with a succession of contrasted ideas. But it isn't the details that matter. The important differences between KV
279 and KV 284 have to do with what could be called *formal strategy*; that is, the way in
which the music is organized round the four thematic events that define sonata form.
This involves three main issues, all of which have to do with tonal design.

The first issue concerns the way in which the music moves to the second key—in both
cases the dominant—and the way in which this move is linked to the second subject.

- KV 284 is more conventional in this respect. In bars 13–21 there is a passage of increasing harmonic tension over a stepwise bass, relaxing onto an elaborated dominant

Ex. 99 Mozart, Sonata KV 284, first movement

Ex. 99 *cont.*

Ex. 99 *cont.*

Ex. 99 *cont.*

Ex. 100

IV - - - - - - - - - - - - - - -V

pedal (G–A–B–B♭–A, **Example 100**). Then there is a break before the second subject, which simply continues in A major (bar 22). So here the second subject marks the arrival at the second key; there is some quite intense harmonic motion in the remainder of the exposition (including a passage built on a transposed version of the G–A–B–B♭–A motif, bars 30–4), but no serious suggestion of any other key.

- In KV 279 there is again a break before the second subject, at bar 16, but this time there has been no move towards the dominant. It is the second subject itself that accomplishes this, by means of a cycle of fifths (E–A–D–G). To compensate for this comparatively late arrival at the new key, the remainder of the exposition revolves almost obsessively round II, V, and I of G major.

The second issue is the way in which the development section is designed to lead to the return of the first subject in the tonic.

- Here KV 279 is more conventional. As Koch would put it, the development section 'dissects' materials from the exposition; that is, it extracts short segments and repeats them in different transpositions. As **Example 101** shows, the entire section works from the bottom up. Like the modulating passage of J. C. Bach's sonata (see Example 95), it is supported by a bass line that moves at first by step, and then by fifths. Finally the music arrives at a dominant pedal, and it simply stays there (decorating it with passage-work and, at the end, a kind of *Eingang*) until the recapitulation.

Ex. 101

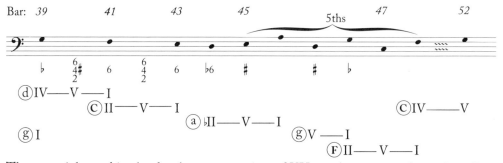

- The materials used in the development section of KV 284, by contrast, have virtually nothing in common with the rest of the movement. (Of course you can *always* find things in common. In particular, the pattern at bar 52, with its parallel sixths and upper pedal, is reminiscent of bars 30–2. But Mozart has avoided making obvious links between the sections.) As in KV 279, the section begins in the minor mode of the dominant key. But the first part of it, up to bar 59, is not supported by a conjunct bass line. As **Example 102** shows, it relies for its continuity upon a series of loose sequences that outline IV–V–I patterns in E minor and B minor. After that, there is a rapid motion through F♯ minor, E minor, and D minor, this time supported by a conjunct bass (bars 62–6). And from here there is a simply a series of chords moving by falling thirds (from D minor to B♭ major, G minor, and E♭ major). The scheme of all this is clear in a mathematical sense: successive movements by fifths (A–E–B–F♯), seconds

Ex. 102

(F#–E–D), and thirds (D–B♭–G–E♭), with the timescale getting progressively shorter. But the *musical* result is complete tonal disorientation. At the beginning of bar 69, where there is a first inversion E♭ chord, there is no sense of an impending return to the tonic. And yet this is suddenly achieved on the last beat of the bar, by a kind of sleight of hand, with each note of the chord moving by step. Unlike in KV 279, then, the recapitulation of KV 284 comes like a bolt out of the blue.

The final issue has to do with precisely this: the way the return of the B section is handled. More generally, it is a question of how the recapitulation is altered as against the exposition.

• KV 284 illustrates just how simple Mozart's practice can be. The recapitulation is hardly changed at all, except of course for the transposition of the B section to the tonic. Even this is achieved with minimum fuss: the music simply continues in the tonic at bar 93, where it had previously continued in the dominant. Apart from this, there are only two changes worth mentioning. First, the repeat of the second subject, at bar 99, is an octave higher (from here to the end, Mozart transposes up a fourth rather than down a fifth), and an extra bar is inserted at 98 in order to get there. And second, an extra four bars are inserted near the end in order to make the ending more conclusive (bars 118–21).

• KV 279 *could* have been just as simple as KV 284. Mozart could perfectly well have repeated the A section from the exposition without alteration, and then gone straight on to the B section transposed to the tonic. (Try playing from bar 1 to the first beat of bar 16, followed by bar 70.) But he chose not to do this. Instead, he rewrote the recapitulation, incorporating most of the original materials but changing the order. The following table summarizes the relationship between the exposition and the recapitulation.

Exposition	*Recapitulation*	
1–4	58–61	same
5–8	62–5	same material but adapted tonally
—	66–7	continuation of above
13–14	68–9	same (but transposed up then down)
17–23	70–8	similar but slightly extended
—	79–80	extra repetition of 75–6 (lower 8ve)
24–25:2	80:3–81	same, transposed down
—	82–84:2	arpeggios as at 9, different harmony
14:3–16:1	84:3–86:1	same
25:2–38:2	86:2–99:2	same (but transposed up then down)
—	99:3–100	new

The freedom with which Mozart chops and changes his materials, butting one against another and re-ordering them, is a reflection of their self-contained, modular nature.

But *why* does he make all these changes in KV 279? One perfectly valid answer is, why not? But there is another answer. The main effect of the changes is to create a passage of harmonic tension shortly after the beginning of the recapitulation. At bar 62 the music moves towards the subdominant, and from there it passes through a series of diminished sevenths before emerging on to the dominant at bar 67. This creates a kind of formal dissonance, in relation to which the resumption of the second subject functions as a kind of resolution. It heightens the drama of what is really only a continuation of the tonic. You might almost say that it creates a modulation from tonic to tonic.

All of this makes excellent musical sense. But in that case, why didn't Mozart do the same in KV 284? One perfectly valid answer is, why should he? But there is another answer. In KV 279, but not in KV 284, the recapitulation is preceded by a lengthy dominant pedal. Maybe Mozart felt that the tonal drama of KV 279 was in danger of sagging.

ASSIGNMENT 45

Make analytical charts of the first movements of Mozart's KV 279 and KV 284, along the lines of Assignment 43.

ASSIGNMENT 46

Mozart wrote an earlier version of the first movement of KV 284, abandoning it nineteen bars into the development section. **Example 103** *shows the original manuscript; it is transcribed in* **Example 104**. *Compare the two versions of the movement and suggest why Mozart abandoned the earlier version.*

ASSIGNMENT 47

Example 105 *is the first half of a sonata movement by Antonio Soler, a Spanish composer who died in 1783. The original is in a fully-fledged sonata form, as described in this chapter. Try to reconstruct it. As in Assignment 43, there is no need to write out all the music that is simply transposed from the first half, but you should say whether it is to be transposed up or down.*

One of the distinguishing features of Classical music is the diversity of styles and textures that it frequently encompasses within a single composition. Even so, there are few pieces in the repertory that exhibit such a kaleidoscopic succession of diverse materials as the first movement from KV 284. Every few bars the music completely changes its character. It's almost as if fragments of a dozen different compositions had been skilfully woven into a single, continuous fabric. Nowadays we tend to look at these things abstractly: we talk of contrasts of texture, articulation, or harmonic rhythm. But it's likely that an eighteenth-century musician would have seen them in a quite different way.

Ex. 103 Autograph of KV 284, with abandoned version

Sonata

Ex. 104

Ex. 104 *cont.*

Ex. 105 Soler, sonata movement, first part. Reproduced by permission of Unión Musical Ediciones, S.L.

Ex. 105 *cont.*

In Chapter 3 I mentioned how eighteenth-century theorists thought of the compositional process in terms of *inventio* and *dispositio*. These weren't in origin musical terms at all; they were drawn from the study of rhetoric, as expounded by such Roman writers as Cicero and Quintilian. (Hence the use of Latin terminology.) These ancient authors classified the various figures of speech, and tried to show how a skilful orator could weave them into a coherent and persuasive argument. Such theories of rhetoric were highly influential among eighteenth-century musicians, who accordingly looked for musical equivalents of figures of speech. They found them in conventional associations and topical references. In their music, Classical composers evoked the many different courtly or rustic dances of the day (of which the minuet was just one); they evoked the sounds of hunting horns and bagpipes. They alluded to the distinctive national styles of music, such as Italian, French, and German. They referred to the various musical genres from military band to opera, and the different performance styles characteristic of each. And they wove all these topical references into a richly variegated fabric, a kind of tapestry of life.

As you might expect, the rediscovery of such period conceptions is largely the work of Leonard Ratner, and one of the pieces he has particularly looked at from this point of view is KV 284. Here is his analysis of part of the first movement:

Bar		
1		orchestral unison as a concerto tutti
4	(left hand)	murky bass
	(right hand)	singing style
7		brilliant style
9	(left hand)	trommel-bass
	(right hand)	singing style
13		orchestral tutti; *concitato*
17		march
21		fanfare
22		singing style; ornamental *stile legato*
25		brilliant style
28		rubato
30		tutti-solo
33		rubato
34		*recitative obligé*
36		brilliant style
38		fanfare
40		singing style
41		fanfare
43		singing style
44		orchestral unison
45		*coups d'archet*
46		singing style
48		fanfare
50		orchestral unison

Most of these terms are self-explanatory; they embrace the whole panoply of Classical instrumental and vocal styles and genres. If Ratner is right, a Classical listener would have heard each of these passages as evoking a particular kind of music, a particular context, a particular mood. He or she would have heard the music modulating, so to speak, from one sound-world to another, and would have followed the resulting pattern of repetitions and cross-references.

It is impossible to cover so complex a subject properly in a few paragraphs, or to give a full lexicon of what Ratner sees as the referential language of Classical music. But even a cursory glance at Ratner's analysis suggests a world of signification that lies hidden behind the sound of Mozart's music. Mozart was not simply a creator of compositional structures, an engineer in sound. His music resonates with lived experience. It is a theatre of the imagination.

CHAPTER 12

A Sonata in the Making

WHENEVER we think of composers' sketches, we think of Beethoven. There are two reasons for this. The first is that Beethoven sketched a great deal—much more than Mozart, for example. (The abandoned version of KV 284 reproduced in the last chapter isn't a sketch; it's a final draft that went wrong.) Whereas Mozart worked out his music largely in his head, Beethoven liked to *see* what he was doing. He seems to have improvised on paper the way most composers improvise at the piano. There are pages in the 'Kafka Miscellany'—a collection of sketch materials, now in the British Library, that go back to the late 1780s—that are filled with patterns of figuration, or miniature dances, that could hardly have been intended for finished compositions. They look much more like the written equivalent of a pianist's limbering-up exercises.

The second reason why we have so many of Beethoven's sketches is that he did not throw them away. He threw away his autographs—that is, scores of completed works, intended for copyists. But he carefully preserved the preparatory sketches. The 'Kafka Miscellany' consists of all sorts of miscellaneous sketches that Beethoven later bound together for safe keeping; when he was working on them, the sketches were on separate leaves. In 1798, however, Beethoven started to use pre-bound sketchbooks. In general he worked through these from beginning to end—though sometimes he jumped from one part of a sketchbook to another, to allow for further work on an earlier project, or ran out of space and turned back to an earlier leaf that was blank.

Despite the complications created by this, and by the dismemberment of some of the sketchbooks after Beethoven's death, it is possible to reconstruct his compositional procedure in a way that is feasible for no other composer before the twentieth century. That is why he is the main source for our knowledge of Classical composers' working methods. There is of course a danger in this. We know so much about how Beethoven composed just because his way of composing was different from everyone else's. This means that studying his sketches is liable to give us a distorted view of the Classical composer's workbench. But that cannot be helped. It is the only close-up view we have.

One of the best known pieces for which there are sketches in the 'Kafka Miscellany' is the little Sonata Op. 49 No. 2. This was written around 1796 or 1797—earlier then the opus number would suggest—and it was probably intended more as a piece for teaching than for public performance. **Example 106** is a facsimile of the surviving sketches for the first movement; **Example 107** is Joseph Kerman's transcription of them. (The little notes above the transcription, such as the *g* in the third stave of Example 107, highlight indistinctly written notes that might represent the adjacent pitch.) Finally, **Example 108** shows the published score.

All the sketches for this movement consist of a single line of music, notated in the treble clef. This is the format in which Beethoven did most of his sketching, though at

Ex. 106 Beethoven, 'Kafka Miscellany', pages 106ʳ and 106ᵛ. Reproduced by permission of the British Library.

Ex. 107 (p. 106r)

Ex. 107 *cont.* (p. 106ᵛ)

Ex. 108 Beethoven, Sonata Op. 49 No. 2, first movement

Ex. 108 *cont.*

Ex. 108 *cont.*

times he would use two or three staves. It was in particular his favoured format for
roughing out large sections of music—as in the first sketch in Example 107 (staves 1–14),
which goes right the way through the exposition and development, as well as showing
the most important parts of the recapitulation. Beethoven scholars call sketches of this
sort *continuity drafts*, and contrast them with other sketches that are concerned with
elaborating thematic or motivic materials. It is obvious that Beethoven was not primarily interested in thematic details when he was working on this sketch: the second subject (third stave, fourth bar of Example 107) is pretty rudimentary. He was concerned
with the large-scale shaping of the music—with its tonal, rhythmic, and tensional form.
It seems likely that what we have here is Beethoven's first attempt to give a well-defined
shape to a movement that he had already roughed out at the keyboard.

   This sketch is close enough to the finished piece that we can simply go through it
looking for the discrepancies between the two. In the very first bar there is an obvious
discrepancy: the melodic figure is in sixteenth notes instead of triplet eighths, though its
contour is more or less the same as that of the final version. It is easy to see why
Beethoven changed this: the sixteenth-note figure is very awkward for beginners
because of its emphasis on the weak fourth finger (the final version is bad enough in this
respect), and it also encourages too slow a tempo. This is the kind of change that is
purely local in effect; it is a matter of surface detail, not underlying structure. And with
one possible exception, the same applies to all the changes up to the second subject. For

instance, the upbeat motif is missing in bar 8 of the sketch. More significantly, the sketch shows the transitional figure at bar 15 in a form that is much closer to bar 36 of the finished movement (notice the initial rising fifth D–A). In changing this passage, Beethoven made it tighter and more characteristic. But the change is not a structural one; bar 16 remains the same.

As for the one point during this section where structural considerations might come into play, in bar 14, this probably just represents a mistake on Beethoven's part. He began to write out the C#–D figure again, continuing the sequence as in bar 10. Such a sequence would more or less inevitably drive the music back to the tonic, whereas the repetition of the D#–E figure (over a bass that moves from C♮ to C#) is the means for reaching the dominant. Did Beethoven originally intend a different, later move to the dominant, but change his mind as he wrote out this sketch? It is possible. But it seems more likely that he wasn't thinking what he was doing as he wrote this bar, and crossed it out as soon as he realized what he had done. Certainly there is nothing in the handwriting that suggests that Beethoven paused for thought at this point.

The second subject, at bar 21, is quite another matter. As I said, it is rudimentary by comparison with the first subject (in fact the repeated notes and syncopations when it is repeated, in stave 4, seem positively banal), and at first sight it has little in common with the finished version. Yet there are a number of similarities between the two versions. Right at the beginning there is a rhythmic similarity, with the three initial eighth notes leading to quarter notes. Both versions have a lot of repeated notes, and they share a similar contour, rising to the high A, before ending on an imperfect cadence. Their phrase structure is similar, too, including a transposed repetition of the initial two-bar phrase. And on the larger scale, there is the repetition of the entire eight-bar thematic unit, with the elision of the final bar of the repeat so that the second subject as a whole occupies 8 + 7 bars. In this way, while the sketch contains hardly any of the *notes* of the final version of the second subject, it embodies most of its significant structural features.

There are two other points in this sketch where significant structural issues are involved. One is in stave 11 of Example 107, after the letters 'd.c.' (which have been added by Kerman). My **Example 109** gives an impression of what may have been intended here. In this version the first subject area is considerably longer in the recapitulation than it was in the exposition. By deleting all this material in the final version of the recapitulation, Beethoven gave his movement a tauter, more directed form.

Ex. 109

The other is the development section, which—despite its name—is the least developed section in the sketch. (It begins on stave 10.) Here it is difficult to be sure quite what is intended; **Example 110** represents one way of reading the passage. It begins in the same manner as the final version (allowing of course for the difference in the first subject), and with the same three-bar phrases. Kerman even reads the the second phrase as beginning on A minor, as in the final version. In Example 110, however, I have changed Kerman's A and C to G and B, so that the phrase begins in E minor. The E minor gives a IV–V progression in B minor, corresponding to the progression of the first phrase; this makes far more musical sense than the A minor Kerman shows.

Ex. 110

But what possible justification can we have for changing what Beethoven wrote? This sounds like a powerful objection, but the concept 'what Beethoven wrote' is not as straightforward as it seems. Look at Example 106: like all Beethoven's sketches, it was written in haste and for his own eyes only. It was not intended as public document (in the way that even the scrappiest autograph was). Because of this, Beethoven could afford to omit things like accidentals, key signatures, and even clefs, and to place his noteheads very inaccurately. And this means that what we are interested in is not what Beethoven *wrote*, but what he *meant* by what he wrote. Another way of putting this is that you cannot simply read sketches like this: you have to interpret them. You have to make your own judgements about what they say. Of course, there is a danger of circularity here: you see what you expect to see. But again, this cannot be helped. It is the only way in which we can possibly understand what Beethoven did.

There is no correspondence between the remainder of the development section and the final version in a bar-to-bar sense—even though the actual number of bars is the same in each case. There are, however, a number of general features shared by both versions. There is the same movement from the opening D minor via a cycle of rising fifths to B; then, at the end of the section, there is a corresponding series of falling fifths (though this is abbreviated to A–D–G in the sketch). There is the same rhythm of a quarter note preceded by an eighth-note upbeat. There is the same repetitiveness and quality of harmonic stasis. As sketched, then, the development section contains little of the actual music of the final version, but it embodies most of its important musical attributes. It clarifies what is needed at this point, even though it doesn't actually provide it.

What is the most important lesson to be drawn from the study of Beethoven's sketches? It is, once again, that you do not write music one note at a time. Beethoven spent inordinate amounts of time establishing musical *contexts*. His formidable powers of melodic and harmonic invention came fully into play only when he had a clear sense of where the music was going—of its form and tonal direction. He needed a vision of the whole before he could refine the details.

ASSIGNMENT 48

Trace the evolution of the first movement of Op. 49 No. 2 through the later sketches in Examples 106 and 107. In order fully to understand this evolution, you will need to have a good analytical grasp of the music; a discussion of the movement, organized round a series of questions about formal strategy, may be found in my Guide to Musical Analysis, *pp. 264–79.*

ASSIGNMENT 49

Example 111 shows another sonata first movement which Beethoven sketched around 1797, also from the 'Kafka Miscellany'; Example 112 is Kerman's transcription (with the addition of bar numbers). This time, Beethoven left the piece unfinished. It is impossible to know how it would have ended up if he had finished it—probably quite different—but it is possible to make a reasonably plausible reconstruction of the movement as Beethoven conceived it at this point, using the sketches and finished version of Op. 49 No. 2 as a model. In doing this, you may like to bear the following points in mind:

- *Bar 3: the sequential opening, with tonic followed by supertonic, is one of the clichés of later Classical sonata style; see, for instance, Mozart's Sonata in D major, KV. 576.*
- *Bar 6: imitation is one way of creating motion here.*
- *Bar 7: do you agree with Kerman's transcription of this bar?*
- *Bar 10: remember that register is necessarily compressed in a one-stave sketch.*
- *Bars 13–17: a strong bass is the key to the harmonic progression here.*
- *Bar 21: why the complex notation here, with rests and noteheads tailed in different directions?*
- *Bar 28: '2temal Var[iert]' means 'varied the second time'. The variation could, of course, be in the accompaniment rather than the tune.*

- *Bar 31: 'usw' means 'and so on'.*
- *Bar 34: the problem here is to inject some harmonic motion. Virtually the only solution is V–IV⁶–V–IV⁶ in C minor.*
- *Bar 35: the gaps between phrases suggest contrapuntal treatment.*
- *Bar 38: some modification to Kerman's transcription is required here.*
- *Bar 39: in this and the following bars, remember that Beethoven's notation of accidentals in the sketchbooks was often casual.*
- *Bar 42: will any previous material fit above this bass line?*
- *Bar 44: the ♯ is to be understood in terms of figured bass notation. (The implication is that the harmony of this bar is $^{6-5}_{4-3}$.)*
- *Bars 45–9: see the remarks under bars 6 and 41 above.*
- *Final stave: 'Schluss' means 'ending' or 'coda'.*

(Of course, the bar numbers of your reconstruction will be different after bar 28.)
Write a short report to accompany your reconstruction of the movement, outlining some of the problems you encountered, and setting the work into its stylistic context.

ASSIGNMENT 50

Choose any sonata first movement by Beethoven, and write an analysis of it.

Ex. III Beethoven, 'Kafka Miscellany' page 149ʳ. Reproduced by permission of the British Library

Ex. 112

Conclusion

IN Chapter 12 I offered some hypothetical reconstructions of what Beethoven may have had in mind during the composition of Op. 49 No. 2, basing these reconstructions on what he wrote in the sketches. In general, the more the sketches differ from the final version of the music, the more this kind of compositional reconstruction becomes a necessary part of their interpretation. And this applies most of all when the work that Beethoven was sketching remained incomplete, whether because of his death (as in the case of the Tenth Symphony), or because he decided to abandon it.

One of the works which he sketched extensively but then abandoned is what would, if completed, have been the Sixth Piano Concerto; there is a forty-page full score of the first (and only) movement, as well as a large number of sketches. The full score, which dates from 1814–15, begins confidently enough, but as it proceeds it becomes increasingly patchy. The orchestration, at first complete, degenerates into little more than a melody and a bass line, with the addition where appropriate of a skeletal piano part. There are gaps, and increasingly there are sections that have been heavily crossed out, often without any indication of what should replace them. And sometimes there are two or even three versions of the music written on top of each other, or rather squeezed into the space left at the beginning and end of a bar, or between the previously-written notes.

It is the last of these that present the biggest headache for anyone trying to make sense of the score as Beethoven left it. You can see that there are incompatible versions of the music, but how do you work out which layer of correction or emendation goes with which? Simply writing down what you see in the score is useless; you end up with gibberish. (Usually it is hard enough to be sure what the notes are, let alone how they fit together.) The only way to make sense of what you see is to follow through the consequences of one reading or another, teasing out its compositional potential. By trying to bring the music into a performable state—trying to make sense of it harmonically, trying to find a bass line to fit it, trying to shape its motion towards the cadence—you test the implications of your interpretation. You take responsibility for your reading of the score. Under such conditions, the kind of composer's-eye view of Classical music that I've tried to give in this book becomes an essential component of the musicological toolkit.

Not everyone wants to learn how to read Beethoven sketches, of course. And you don't need a composer's-eye view to enjoy listening to Classical music. But the ability to see the music from the inside—to understand it in period terms, to follow the composer's strategy as he negotiates its structure—is what marks out a specifically musicianly way to hear Classical music. (It is the best foundation for articulate performance, too. But that's something I don't have space to enlarge upon in this book.) Moreover, this composer's-eye view is largely transferable from Classical music with a capital 'C'—the music of J. C. Bach, Haydn, Mozart, Beethoven—to classical music in the broader sense, by which I mean the common-practice repertory from Bach to Brahms (and perhaps from Monteverdi to Messiaen). Classical music in the narrow sense represents an unusually transparent musical style in which the technical principles common to the common-practice repertory stand out in relief: the two-part framework of melody and bass, the mutual relationship of harmony and line, motion towards a goal and cadential structure, variation, expansion, and prolongation.

But there's another and deeper sense in which these technical principles are transferable. In this book, I have repeatedly stressed the analytical component of Classical musicianship—the way in which arrangement, or accompaniment, or writing variations, or expanding small forms into large ones, involves deciding what goes with what, and what is more important than what. The modular principle of expansion involves locating what I called the break points in the music—that is, it is based on what theorists call *segmentation*. Accompaniment involves deciding which melody notes form a group corresponding to a single harmony; it is based on *association*. Arrangement and the writing of variations involve stripping off the musical surface in order to arrive at its underlying melodic and harmonic structure; they are based on *reduction*. In each case, the theoretical concept can be applied to the Classical context, but is far more general in its scope: the concepts of segmentation, association, and reduction can be applied in a host of different ways and to the broadest range of the world's musics.

The practice of Classical composition, then, lays the foundations for the more abstract, and consequently more powerful, concepts of music theory. The reading list offers some suggestions as to how to build on these foundations.

Further Reading

- I have discussed the role of reconstruction in sketch study at greater length, and with illustrations, in 'A Performing Edition of Beethoven's Sixth Piano Concerto?', *Beethoven Newsletter*, 8/3–9/1 (1994), 71–80. (An account of the concerto itself may be found in my article 'Beethoven's Unfinished Piano Concerto: a Case of Double Vision?', *Journal of the American Musicological Society*, 42 (1989), 338–74.)
- Single-volume introductions to analysis, covering a range of methods, include Jonathan Dunsby and Arnold Whittall's *Music Analysis in Theory and Practice* (London and New Haven, 1988) and Ian Bent's *Analysis* (London and New York, 1987), as well as my *Guide to Musical Analysis* (London and New York, 1987). For Schenkerian analysis see also Allen Forte and Steven Gilbert's *Introduction to Schenkerian Analysis* (New York, 1982), and David Neumeyer and Susan Tepping's *A Guide to Schenkerian Analysis* (Englewood Cliffs, NJ, 1992).

A checklist of Classical Harmony

The basic resources of Classical harmony are as follows:

	Diatonic	Chromatic	
TRIADS	I		*Tonic*
		♭II	*Neapolitan sixth*, so called because normally in $\frac{6}{3}$ position. Dominant approach chord.
	II		*Supertonic*
	III		*Mediant*
	IV		*Subdominant*
	V		*Dominant.* Major triad (i.e. incorporates raised $\hat{7}$ in minor mode).
		♭VI	*Flattened submediant.* Applies to major mode only.
	VI		*Submediant*
	VII		*Leading note chord* (i.e. on raised $\hat{7}$ in minor mode). Semi-independent chord, often assimilated to V^7.
SEVENTHS	V^7		*Dominant seventh*
	others^7		*Secondary sevenths.* Dominant approach chords or in chains of sevenths.
		any^{o7}	*Diminished seventh* chords. Act as substitutes for V^7 or as passing chords.
OTHER		♭VI$^{\#6}$	VI$^{\#6}$ in minor mode. *Augmented sixth* chord; normally in root position. Dominant approach chord.

INVERSIONS All the above are used in any inversion, except as stated, and except for second inversions, of which only V^6_4 is generally used:

- *cadential six-four.* Dominant approach chord, e.g. II^6–V^{6-5}_{4-3}–I
- *passing six-four.* V chord in second inversion, linking I and I^6.

CADENCES
- V–I (*perfect or full cadence*)
- I–V, II–V, IV–V (*imperfect or half cadence*)
- V–VI (*interrupted cadence*). Less common.
- IV–I (*plagal cadence*). Rare.

Although many other combinations of notes are found, these are in almost all cases best understood as elaborations of these basic harmonies, resulting from:

- passing notes or chords
- neighbour notes or chords
- appoggiaturas

- suspensions
- pedal notes
- chromatic alteration

APPENDIX 2

Instrumental Ranges

The following are typical ranges within which Classical composers wrote. They are not the total ranges of modern instruments; they are not the total ranges available on Classical instruments. They are merely a rough guide to typical usage. Ranges refer to written, not sounding, pitch (this affects only the clarinet). For brass instruments see Chapter 1, Example 21.

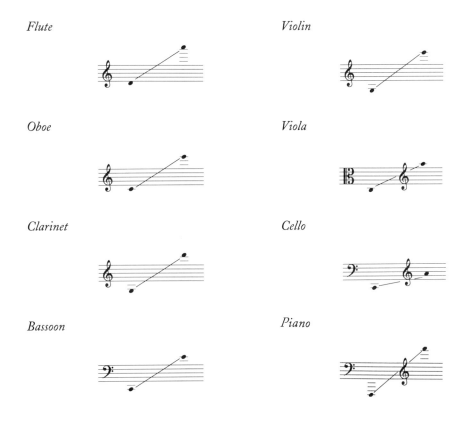

Glossary

*Words included in the Glossary are printed in **bold italics** on their first appearance in the main text.*

Appoggiatura. A type of *non-harmony note*; essentially an accented upper *neighbour note* (that is, one that occurs on the beat). Thus all appoggiaturas are neighbour notes, but not all neighbour notes are appoggiaturas.

Augmented sixth chord. A *triad* to which a sharpened sixth has been added, e.g. C–E–G–A♯; most often found on ♭VI (VI in minor mode), where it functions as a dominant approach.

Binary. Divided into two main sections. Used primarily to distinguish binary forms from *ternary* ones.

Cadence. A harmonic and melodic stopping point, which defines the *phrase* of which it forms part. Cadences are traditionally categorized into four types on the basis of harmony: *perfect* or *full* (V–I), *imperfect* or *half* (anything–V), *interrupted* or *deceptive* (V–VI), and *plagal* (IV–I), of which the last is infrequent in Classical music. However these and other labels are used in an inconsistent manner, and it is often easier just to spell out the Roman letters (e.g. a V–I cadence).

Cantus firmus. A given melody, normally in long notes, around which a contrapuntal texture is constructed, with the other parts moving more rapidly. For the Classical composers, a throwback to Renaissance style, which they saw in the light of *strict counterpoint*.

Chromatic. Using any note that does not belong to the scale of the current key. The opposite of diatonic.

Chromatic alteration. Raising or lowering a note by changing the accidental.

Close position. A chord is in close position when its different notes are as close together as possible, for instance c¹–e¹–g¹. The opposite is *open position*, for instance c¹–g¹–e². (For the meaning of the superscript numbers, see *register*.)

Closed A *phrase* or other section of music that does not demand continuation is closed. This usually means that it ends on I of the *home key*.

Conjunct. Proceeding by step, that is in a series of seconds. The opposite is *disjunct*.

Consonance. A note, chord, or key that is regarded as stable. In Classical music, the only fully consonant chord (i.e. capable of being used as a final chord) is the tonic *triad*.

Consonant skip. The movement of a line from one harmony note to another. A series of consonant skips constitutes an arpeggio.

Contour. The overall shape of a melody considered in terms of up and down.

Contrary motion. See *parallel* motion.

Counterpoint, contrapuntal. Texture made up of independent lines. Opposite of homophony.

Cross or **false relation.** When the same note appears with different accidentals in different parts but in close proximity; common in the sixteenth century, but normally avoided in Classical music.

Cycle of fifths. Commonly-used progression in which the *roots* of successive chords are related by perfect or diminished fifths. Such progressions may stay within one key or move between keys.

Diatonic. Using only the notes that belong to the scale of the current key. The opposite of chromatic.

Diminished seventh chord. See *seventh chord*.

Dissonance. A note, chord, or key that is regarded as unstable and requiring *resolution*.

Dominant preparation. Passage leading to a structural dominant, usually serving to heighten dramatic tension.

Double stop refers to playing two strings at once on a violin or similar instrument. Similarly *triple* and *multiple* stops. See Chapter 1, p. 25.

Downbeat. The strongest beat in a bar, i.e. the first beat; the term is sometimes used by analogy on a larger scale (e.g. for the beginning of a phrase).

Elision. When the beginning of one phrase (or any melodic or rhythmic unit) also functions as the end of the previous one.

Fermata. A pause, generally but not necessarily at the point of cadence.

Figured bass. Shorthand system for indicating harmonies to be added to a bass line, explained in Chapter 2.

Harmonic rhythm. The rhythm created by changing harmonies. Classical music tends to have a slow and regular harmonic rhythm (typically with one or two harmonies per bar), coupled with rapid and sometimes irregular surface rhythms.

Harmony note. A note that belongs to the current harmony. The opposite of a *non-harmony note*.

Home key. The overall *tonic* of a movement—that is, the key in which it begins and ends.

Homophony, **homophonic.** Texture made up of chords rather than independent lines. Opposite of counterpoint.

Imitation. The echoing of a melodic or rhythmic pattern between one line and another; an extremely common device in baroque music (for instance Bach's Two-Part Inventions) and in *contrapuntal* music generally. Where a whole line is echoed, rather than just a single pattern, the term 'imitation' is not used—the correct word would be 'canon' or 'fugue'.

Imperfect. See *cadence*.

Interrupted. See *cadence*.

Inversion. This refers to the *registers* in which the notes of a chord occur. A *triad* is in *root position* when its lowest note is the *root*, in *first inversion* when the lowest note is the third, and in *second inversion* when the lowest note is the fifth. Inversions are often referred to in terms of figured bass, thus root position is $\frac{5}{3}$, first inversion is $\frac{6}{3}$, and second inversion is $\frac{6}{4}$. All the foregoing refers to *harmonic inversion*; *melodic inversion* simply means turning a tune upside down (i.e. substituting rising for falling intervals, and vice versa).

Melisma. An expressive melodic elaboration. The term is especially associated with Gregorian chant, where it means the elaboration of a single syllable, but it may be applied to music in any style.

Modulate, modulation. Moving from one key to another. See Chapter 4.

Motif or **motive.** A characteristic melodic fragment, defined by its pitches or its rhythm or both.

Neapolitan. Refers to the major triad on the flattened supertonic (♭II), generally used as a cadential approach chord (♭II–V). Since it is usually in first inversion (i.e. a $\frac{6}{3}$ chord) is sometimes called the 'Neapolitan sixth'.

Neighbour note. A *non-harmony note* that decorates a single *harmony note* (rather than linking two harmony notes, as in the case of the *passing note*). Neighbour notes include *suspensions* and *appoggiaturas* as well as auxiliary notes, escape notes, anticipations, and cambiatas.

Non-harmony note. A note which does not belong to the current harmony. See *passing note*, *neighbour note*, *suspension*, *pedal note*.

Open. A *phrase* or other section of music is open when it demands continuation—for instance, when it ends on any chord other than I.

Open position. See *close position*.

Parallel motion generally refers to two or more lines that stay a fixed interval apart from one another. Parallel thirds and sixths are commonplace features of the Classical style. Parallel fifths and octaves were generally avoided, at least between outer parts (except, in the case of octaves, when used as a special effect). Parallel chords are more or less restricted to first inversion triads. The term 'parallel motion' is also used in a less precise way to refer to two lines (e.g. a melody and bass) that both move up or down, regardless of the specific intervals between them; in this sense it is the opposite of *contrary motion*.

Part-writing. Refers to the manner of handling the relationships between different musical lines. For the conventions of Classical part-writing see Chapter 1, p. 18.

Passing chord, passing harmony. The same idea as *passing note*, but applied at the level of chords; a chord or series of chords linking two structural harmonies.

Passing note. A *non-harmony note* linking two *harmony notes* in a single stepwise motion (e.g. C–D–E, E–D–C over C major harmony).

Pedal note. Otherwise known as 'pedal point' or simply 'pedal'. A note which is held regardless of the surrounding harmonies, generally but not always in the bass. The term derives from the organ.

Perfect. See *cadence*.

Period. A larger section than a *phrase*, typically consisting of two phrases. Like 'phrase', this is not a precise term.

Phrase. The smallest unit in music that makes a complete, coherent gesture; usually about four bars long and ending with a cadence. It is not a precise term.

Pivot chord. A chord that is used in relation to more than one key in the course of *modulation* (e.g. a C chord functioning simultaneously as I of C and IV of G). See Chapter 4, p. 54.

Plagal. See *cadence*.

Reduction. The analytical process or product of picking out the most important notes from a piece of music in order to determine its underlying organization.

Register. Refers to how high or low a note is; thus middle C is in a higher register than the C an octave below. The audible pitch range is conventionally divided into octave bands, each running from C to the B above. There are a number of systems for designating into which band a note falls. The most common is to represent middle C as 'c¹', with the next C up being 'c²', the following one 'c³', and so on; the C below middle C is 'c', the one below that 'C', and the one below *that* 'C¹'. This is a source of confusion, since 'C' may equally well mean the C two octaves below middle C, or any C regardless of register. You have to tell which is intended from the context.

Resolve, resolution. Unstable formations (*dissonances*) resolve to stable ones (*consonances*). The term can be used at any level from a single note to a key.

Roman letters or **numerals.** System of analysing chord relationships based on the relationship of the *root* of each chord to the *tonic*; see the Introduction, p. 4. In this book, I use only upper-case letters (I, II, etc), which refer to major, minor, or diminished triads according to the context (thus in a major key I is a major triad, II is a minor triad, etc.). Other writers distinguish I (major triad) from i (minor triad), and add symbols to identify augmented (I⁺) and diminished (i°) triads. Roman letters were first used around 1800, but their widespread adoption dates from the middle of the nineteenth century.

Root position. See *inversion*.

Root. Generating note of a triad or other chord, defined as its lowest note when the chord is arranged as a stack of thirds (thus the root of the C major triad C–E–G is C).

Scale degree. A way of referring to the different notes of the scale, counting from the **root** which is 1. Carets (î) are sometimes used to indicate that it is scale degrees to which the numbers refer.

Secondary dominant. A V chord which is not itself diatonic to the main key, but is the dominant of a chord which *is*. So, for instance, V of V (in C major, a D major chord) is a secondary dominant.

Sequence. Repetition of a short musical passage, normally within the same key but beginning on a different *scale degree*. (A sequence is therefore an instance of tonal **transposition**.)

Seventh chord. *Triad* with a seventh added. By far the most common is the dominant seventh (V⁷), which functions as an intensified version of the standard V. The catch-all term *secondary seventh* is used for all other sevenths. A special case is the *diminished seventh*, which consists of four notes a minor third apart (e.g. C–E♭–F♯–A); these generally appear as **passing chords**, but sometimes function similarly to dominants.

Sonata. Instrumental composition for one or more instruments; in the Classical period normally in three movements, but sometimes less or more. See Chapters 10–12.

Sonata form. A term introduced in the middle of the nineteenth century to describe the typical structure of first movements in Classical sonatas and symphonies; nowadays the term is used with considerable caution. See the Introduction to Section IV.

Strict or **species counterpoint.** A system of composition teaching codified by Johann Fux in 1725. It was based on the Palestrina style (or what Fux thought of as the Palestrina style) and the basic technique it taught was elaborating simple, consonant formations into complex, dissonant ones. As well as being a pedagogical device, it helped mould the Classical composers' conception of early music, and their own music is full of 'topical' references to it. See Chapter 6, p. 84.

Strophic. A strophic song is one in which the same music is used for each verse. The opposite is *through-composed*.

Subject. A term used in traditional formal analysis for a characteristic melody that has a special structural role within a movement; it is especially associated with *sonata form*, which is organized round first and second subjects. In the earlier part of this century, sonata form was generally seen in terms of melodic rather than tonal design, and so the terms 'subject' and 'theme' were used more or less interchangeably. Nowadays it is usual to emphasize tonal structure rather than tunes, and people sometimes refer to the first and second 'subject areas' or even 'tonal areas'.

Suspension. A type of **non-harmony note** that occurs when moving from one harmony to another, explained in the Introduction, p. 7.

Syncopation. Throwing the accent off the main beat, so creating a tension between rhythm and metre.

Ternary. Divided into three main sections. Used primarily to distinguish ternary forms from **binary** ones.

Texture. A catch-all term referring to the way in which melodies and harmonies are laid out, best illustrated by means of some of the adjectives that may be applied to it: chordal, linear, contrapuntal, simple, elaborate, widely spaced, bottom-heavy, clear, muddy, smooth, rough. Synonymous with the musical fabric.

Tonic. Tonal centre of a composition or section of a composition, defined as the main note of the predominant key. In practice, the note with the greatest quality of finality. To determine the tonic look at the end of the music (as well as at the key signature when appropriate).

Topics. Characteristic musical types (dances, military music, hunting horns, etc.), frequently evoked in Classical compositions. See Chapter 11, p. 181.

Transposition. Shifting a piece of music up or down, whether by an octave or any other interval. In the latter case, transposition may be *literal* (e.g. C–D–E–D–C becomes D–E–F♯–E–D) or *tonal* (it becomes D–E–F♮–E–D, remaining within the C major scale). Transposing instruments are those for which the pitch as written is different from the pitch as sounded; for instance, when played by a clarinet in B♭, a written C sounds as B♭. (So a B♭ clarinet part has to be written a major second higher than the intended sound.) The only transposing instruments commonly used during the Classical period were the clarinet and brass instruments such as the horn and trumpet (see Chapter 1, p. 25)—apart from the double bass, which sounds an octave below the notation.

Triad. Three-note chord consisting of a *root* plus its third and fifth (thus the C triad is C–E–G). The basic building block of Classical harmony. Triads may be *major* (C–E–G), *minor* (C–E♭–G), *augmented* (C–E–G♯), or *diminished* (C–E♭–G♭).

Triple stop. See *double stop*.

Worksheets

Worksheets are numbered according to the assignment to which they refer.
They may be freely copied.

THERE ARE WORKSHEETS FOR ASSIGNMENTS	
1	14
2	16
3	17
7	18
8	22
9	24
10	25
11	28
12	35
13	36

Analysis through Composition

Worksheet 1

NAME
_____

INSTRUCTOR
_____

DATE _____

Below are bars 5–8 and 29–32 of J. C. Bach's Sonata Op. 5 No. 2 (Example 3).
In each case:

- Ring the non-harmony notes.
- Label them (P or N).
- Add Roman letters wherever the harmony changes.

- Now list the number of times each chord function appears in the whole of bars 1–8.

I: III: V: VII:

II: IV: VI:

Analysis through Composition

Worksheet 2

NAME

_____

INSTRUCTOR

_____

DATE _____

Complete this analysis of bars 29–52 of Example 3.

- Decide where the main sections come and write them in (B1, B2, etc.)
- Write in their length in bars.
- The keys have already been written in. Add Roman letters to show the harmonies on which each main section begins and ends. No other Roman letters are required.
- Finally, add an 'umbrella diagram'.

Bar	29	33	37	41	45	49	
Section	‖:		:‖:				:‖
Length							
Key	d	F			d		
Harmony							

Analysis through Composition
Worksheet 3

NAME

INSTRUCTOR

DATE

• Complete the Roman letter analysis. Then add two violin parts and a cello part.

Menuet

Analysis through Composition

Worksheet 7

NAME

INSTRUCTOR

DATE

Analyse this song by Mozart. First, add slurs above the music to show the phrases. Then identify keys and add Roman letters. When you have completed this:

- List the number of times each chord function appears.

  I: III: V: VII:
  II: IV: VI:

- Classify each cadence (as perfect, imperfect, or interrupted).

  Bar 4:   Bar 28:
  Bar 8:   Bar 32:
  Bar 16:   Bar 36:
  Bar 20:   Bar 40:

Mässig

1. Freu - de,   Kö - ni - gin der Wei - sen,   die,   mit Blu - men

7

um   ihr Haupt,   dich   auf güld' - ner Lei - er___ prei - sen,   ru - hig,

Analysis through Composition

Worksheet 8

NAME

INSTRUCTOR

DATE

• Figure the bass of bars 13–40 of the Mozart song shown below. Your figures should correspond to the editor's realization.

Hö - re— mich von— die - nem Thro - ne, Kind der Weis - heit,

de - ren— Hand im - mer selbst in— dei - ne— Kro - ne ih - re—

schön - sten Ro - sen— band, ih - re— schön - sten Ro - sen band!

Analysis through Composition

Worksheet 9

NAME

_____

INSTRUCTOR

_____

DATE _____

• Complete this realization of a song by Christian Graaf

Laat ons Jui - chen, Ba - ta - vie -ren! Thans ver - rijst d'Or - an -je___ Zon, Die aan't

hoofd   van't Lands - bes - tie - ren, Eer de___ gul-de Vrij-heid won. D'Eers - te

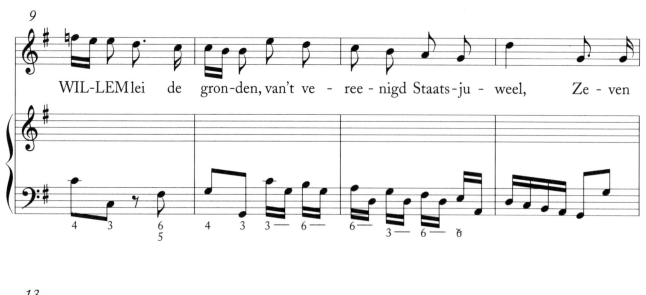

WIL-LEM lei de gron-den, van 't ve - ree - nigd Staats-ju - weel,   Ze - ven

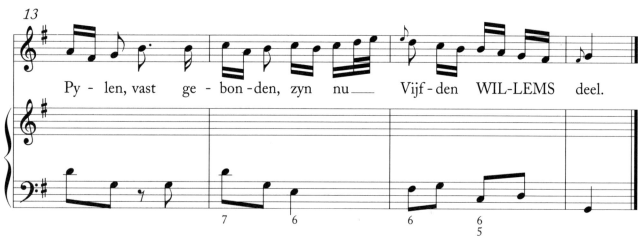

Py - len, vast ge - bon-den, zyn nu___ Vijf-den WIL-LEMS deel.

Analysis through Composition
Worksheet 10

NAME

INSTRUCTOR

DATE

• Complete this realization of a song by Mozart

Langsam

1. O— hei - li-ges Band_ der_ Freund - schaft treu - er Brü - der, dem_

höch - sten_ Glück___ und_ E - dens_Won - ne gleich, dem

Glau — ben_ freund,_ doch nim - mer-mehr zu - wi - der, der_

Welt____ be - kannt___ und___ doch___ ge - heim - nis - reich, ___

Coro

ja, be - kannt___ und___ doch___ ge - heim - nis - reich.

Analysis through Composition

Worksheet 11

NAME _____

INSTRUCTOR _____

DATE _____

• Add a piano accompaniment to 'Sophie's song' by Ignaz Umlauf

Hoff - nung, Lab - sal al - ler__ Mü - den,

mir ist dei - ne__ Macht be - wusst, du gibst al - len

Her - zen__ Frie - den und du bist__ der__ Men - schen Lust.

Analysis through Composition
Worksheet 12

NAME

INSTRUCTOR

DATE

- Analyse these Mozart dance tunes on the model of Example 32.
- Add a bass line to each.

Bar	1	5	9	13
Phrase				
Key				
Begins				
Ends				

Bar	1	5	9	13
Phrase				
Key				
Begins				
Ends				

Analysis through Composition

Worksheet 13

NAME

INSTRUCTOR

DATE

This assignment is in two parts.

- Add labels to the music below to indicate the types of melodic elaboration used in them (P, N, A, or CS).
- Complete the two-part dance shown overleaf. Base your completion on Example 43, which is a reduction of the original music.

Menuet

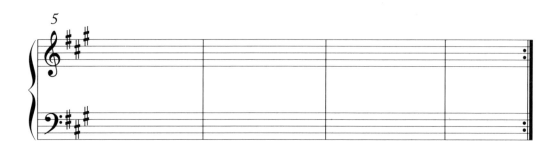

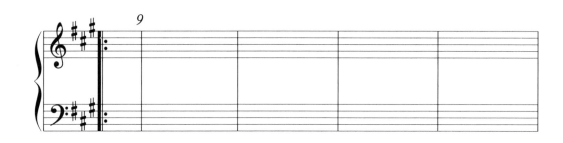

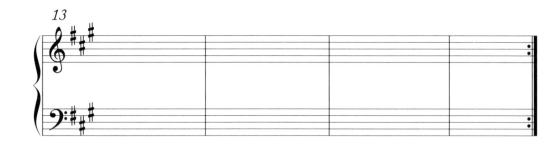

Analysis through Composition
Worksheet 14

NAME

INSTRUCTOR

DATE

• Complete the following sixteen-bar dances for melody instrument and bass.

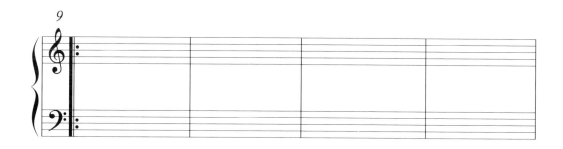

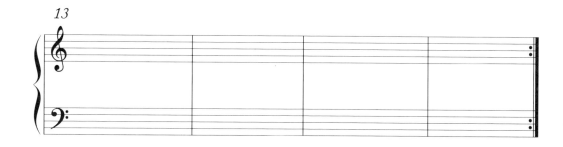

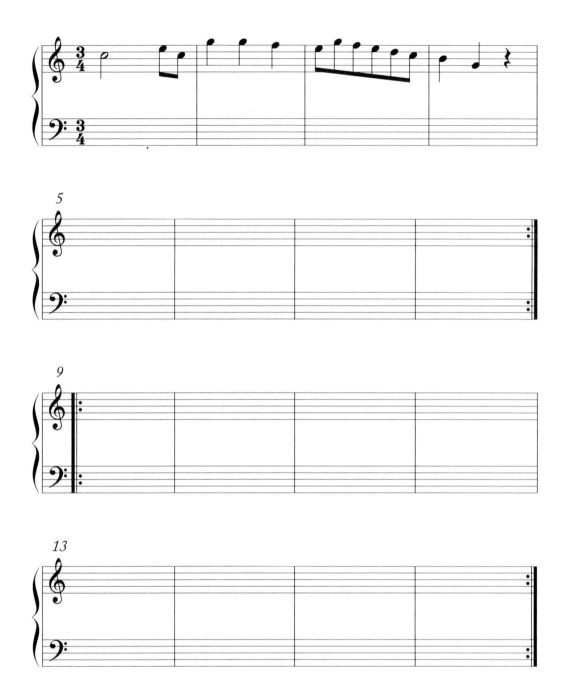

Analysis through Composition

Worksheet 16

NAME

INSTRUCTOR

DATE

This assignment is in two parts.

- Add Roman letters and boxes to the excerpts below, as shown.
- Complete eight alternative versions of bars 9–12 of Example 31, modelling them on the eight passages in Example 45. Use the answer sheet overleaf.

(a) V–V, inflection towards dominant

(b) V–V, modulation to dominant

(c) I⁶–V via II

(d) I⁶–I⁶ via II, with sequence

(e) V–V via VI

(f) V–V via VI, with sequence

(g) I⁶–V via IV

(h) I⁶–V via IV, with sequence

Analysis through Composition
Worksheet 17

NAME

INSTRUCTOR

DATE

This assignment is in two parts.

- The opening for a sixteen-bar dance shown below appeared previously in Assignment 14. Compose another completion of it, this time modulating to V in the second phrase, and passing through other keys in the third.
- Compose a 16-bar dance of your own, passing through a variety of keys. Use the staves overleaf.

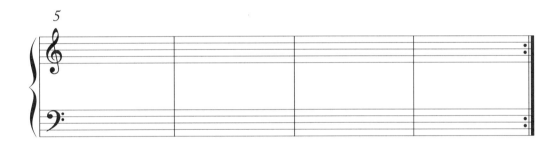

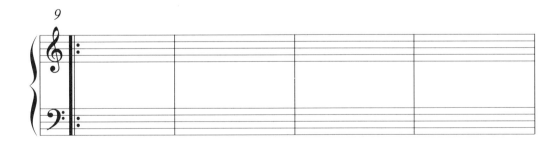

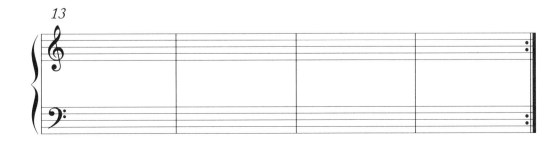

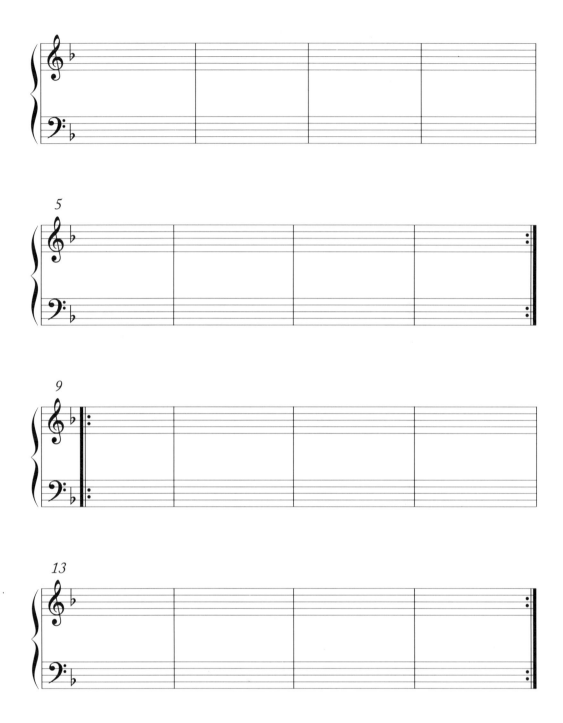

Analysis through Composition
Worksheet 18

NAME

INSTRUCTOR

DATE

• Add a bass line to this minuet by Christian Scheinpflug.

Analysis through Composition

Worksheet 22

NAME

_____

INSTRUCTOR

_____

DATE _____

• Add second violin and viola parts to the following.

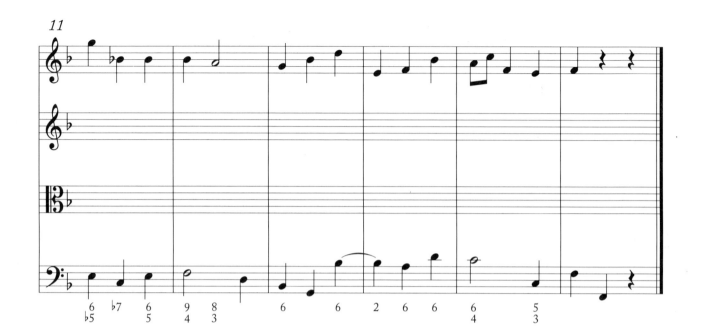

Analysis through Composition

Worksheet 24

NAME

INSTRUCTOR

DATE

• Add second violin and viola parts to the following. Base what you write on Mozart's figures.

Analysis through Composition

Worksheet 25

NAME

INSTRUCTOR

DATE

- Add second violin and viola parts to the following three alternative versions of the first half of a minuet. Base what you write on Mozart's figures.
- Then complete the minuet.

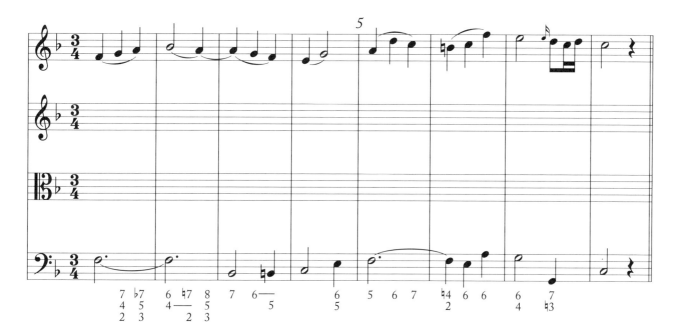

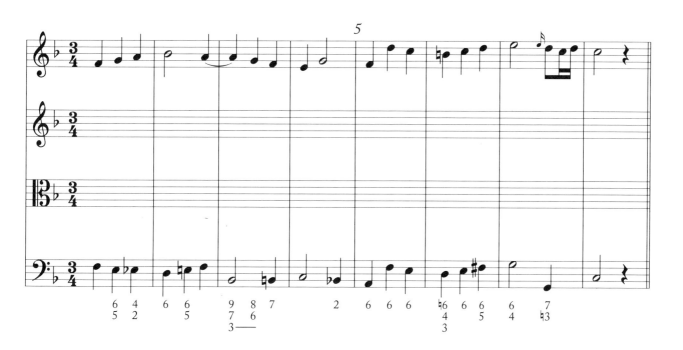

Analysis through Composition

Worksheet 28

NAME

INSTRUCTOR

DATE

- Complete the bass line, moving in quarter notes.
- Then write a bass line in eighth notes, basing it on your previous answer.
- Finally write a bass line in sixteenth notes.

Use your own music paper for the eighth-note and sixteenth-note bass lines.

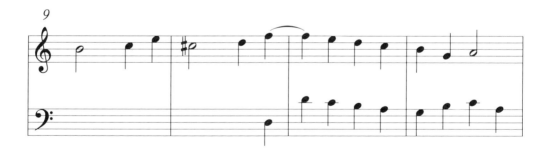

Analysis through Composition

Worksheet 35

NAME

INSTRUCTOR

DATE

This assignment is in two parts.

- Add brackets to pieces (*a*) and (*b*) below and state how the music may be transposed so as to
  1. adapt the first period of (*a*) (up to the double bar) to end in the tonic;
  2. adapt the second period of (*a*) to start in the dominant and end as written;
  3. adapt the first period of (*b*) to end in the dominant;
  4. adapt the second period of (*b*) to begin in E minor and end as written.
- Refer to the text for the second part of this assignment, which is to be answered on your own music paper.

Analysis through Composition

Worksheet 36

NAME

_____

INSTRUCTOR

_____

DATE _____

This assignment is in two parts.

- Below are the original (*a*) and expanded (*b*) versions of the first half of a short piece. Put brackets round the additions to the expanded version, and label the techniques of expansion.
- Overleaf is the first half of a movement by Haydn. It is possible to see it as an expanded sixteen-bar period. Put brackets round the additions.

Allegretto